volume 6 15

Key figures a

(to be used with *Volume 2*)

the complete guide to
Godly Play

Jerome W. Berryman

An imaginative method for presenting scripture stories to children

Illustrations: Brian Dumm, Leslie Dunlap, Victoria Hummel

ISBN: 978-1-9319-6042-7

TABLE OF CONTENTS

*Note: Introductory material special to this volume will be found on pages 10-15, 21-22.

FOREWORD

Special thanks goes to The Reverend Cheryl Minor for dauntless support and hard work on this volume. She is the Rector of All Saints Episcopal Church in Belmont, Massachusetts, a Godly Play Trainer, the Regional Training Coordinator for the North East Region, and a consultant for Morehouse Education Resources, our publisher.

Special mention needs to be made of the Vestry and members of All Saints. This is a church where Godly Play is loved and encouraged. Their support for their Rector concerning this project and all her Godly Play work shows that they know something about the interplay between children and adults, a kind of mutual blessing, that nourishes spiritual maturity. Their spirit is part of this Volume.

Since the first printing of this volume, our publisher, formerly known as Living the Good News, has become Morehouse Education Resources—a division of Church Publishing Incorporated. Morehouse Education Resources will continue to be a leading provider of high quality faith formation resources—including the Godly Play volumes, and the lectionary-based curriculum *Living the Good News*. And, through a new relationship with the Godly Play Foundation, Church Publishing Incorporated has become the exclusive worldwide distributor of Godly Play materials.

James Creasey, the Publisher of Living the Good News, was a friend of this project from the beginning and made it possible for Godly Play to dance out from the pages of the volumes into the middle of circles of children. Thank you, James. The project's editor is Dirk de Vries. He too has been there since the beginning. His sure editing pen has made what is on these pages more clear and able to dance. This has allowed God's Spirit to move in and out of the words.

Many, many, many children have helped with this. There are too many to mention and some I do not even know. Thank you, my friends.

The Godly Play Trainers have contributed more than they know to this project by their work on draft stories and by their many comments. This is a group of people who care about children, God's presence in the midst of their work, and making this as beautiful as it can be.

Above all, I want to thank Thea. We have "talked children" and worked with them all our marriage, which began in 1961. The last two years we have been working with 3-6 year olds, while most of the last several decades we have worked more with people in late childhood and adolescence. Thea's experience and talent as a Montessori music teacher is astounding. Sometimes I go to her class just to watch the magic she creates as children fall in love with music. Thank you, Thea.

Jerome Berryman

INTRODUCTION

Welcome to *The Complete Guide to Godly Play, Volume 6*. In this volume, we gather together fifteen enrichment presentations to be integrated with *Volume 2*. In *Volume 1* of the series, *How to Lead Godly Play Lessons*, there is an in-depth overview of the theory and practice of Godly Play. Below, you'll find only quick reminder notes. Please refer to *Volume 1* to read more about this.

Following this Introduction, you'll find all the information you need to present these enrichment presentations for Fall to the children in your Godly Play room. We hope the simple format will enable all teachers, whether new or experienced, to find the information they need to enter fully into the most rewarding play we share: Godly Play.

WHAT IS GODLY PLAY?

Godly Play is what Jerome Berryman calls his interpretation of Montessori religious education. It is an imaginative approach to working with children, an approach that supports, challenges, nourishes and guides their spiritual quest; it is more akin to spiritual direction than to what we generally think of as religious education.

Godly Play assumes that children have some experience of the mystery of the presence of God in their lives, but that they lack the language, permission and understanding to express and enjoy that in our culture. In Godly Play, we enter into parables, silence, sacred stories and sacred liturgy in order to discover more about God, ourselves, one another and the world around us.

In Godly Play, we prepare a special environment for children to work with adult guides. Two teachers guide the session, making time for the children:
- to enter the space and be greeted
- to get ready for the presentation
- to enter into a presentation based on a parable, sacred story or liturgical action
- to respond to the presentation through shared wondering
- to respond to the presentation (or other significant spiritual issues) with their own work, either expressive art or with the lesson materials
- to prepare and share a feast
- to say goodbye and leave the space

To help understand what Godly Play *is*, we can also take a look at what Godly Play is *not*. First, Godly Play is *not* a complete children's program. Christmas pageants, vacation Bible school, children's choirs, children's and youth groups, parent-child retreats, picnics, service opportunities and other components of a full and vibrant children's ministry are all important and are not in competition with Godly Play.

What Godly Play contributes to the glorious mix of activities is the heart of the matter, the art of knowing—and knowing how to use the language of the Christian people to make meaning of life and death.

Godly Play is different from many other approaches to children's work with scripture. One popular approach is having fun with scripture. That's an approach we might find in many church school pageants, vacation Bible schools or other such suggested children's activities.

Having superficial fun with scripture is fine, but children also need deeply respectful experiences with scripture if they are to fully enter into its power. If we leave out the heart of the matter, we risk trivializing the Christian way of life. We also miss the profound fun of existential discovery, a kind of "fun" that keeps us truly alive!

HOW DO WE DO GODLY PLAY?

When doing Godly Play, *be patient*. With time, your own teaching style, informed by the practices of Godly Play, will emerge. Even if you use another curriculum for church school, you can begin to incorporate aspects of Godly Play into your practice—beginning with elements as simple as the greeting and goodbye.

Pay careful attention to the environment you provide for children. The Godly Play environment is an "open" environment in the sense that children may make genuine choices regarding both the materials they use and the process by which they work toward shared goals. The Godly Play environment is a "boundaried" environment in the sense that children are protected and guided to make constructive choices.

As teachers, we set nurturing boundaries for the Godly Play environment by managing time, space and relationships in a clear and firm way. The setting needs such limits to be the kind of safe place in which a creative encounter with God can flourish. Let's explore each of these in greater depth.

HOW TO MANAGE TIME

AN IDEAL SESSION

In its research setting, a full Godly Play session takes about two hours. An ideal session has four parts, each part echoing the way most Christians organize their worship together.

OPENING: ENTERING THE SPACE AND BUILDING THE CIRCLE

The storyteller sits in the circle, waiting for the children to enter. The door person helps children and parents separate outside the room, and helps the children slow down as they enter the room.

The storyteller helps each child sit in a specific place in the circle, and greets each child warmly by name.

The storyteller, by modeling and direct instruction, helps the children get ready for the day's presentation.

HEARING THE WORD OF GOD: PRESENTATION AND RESPONSE

The storyteller first invites a child to move the hand of the Church "clock" wall hanging to the next block of color. The storyteller then presents the day's lesson. At the presentation's end, the storyteller invites the children to wonder together about the lesson. The storyteller then goes around the circle asking each child to choose work for the day. If necessary, the door person helps children get out their work, either storytelling materials or art supplies. As the children work, some might remain with the storyteller, who presents another lesson to them. This smaller group is made up of those who aren't able to choose work on their own yet.

SHARING THE FEAST: PREPARING THE FEAST AND SHARING IT IN HOLY LEISURE

The door person helps three children set out the feast—such as juice, fruit or cookies—for children to share. Children take turns saying prayers, silently or aloud, until the last prayer is said by the storyteller. The children and storyteller share the feast, then clean things up and put the waste in the trash.

DISMISSAL: SAYING GOODBYE AND LEAVING THE SPACE

The children get ready to say goodbye. The door person calls each child by name to say goodbye to the storyteller. The storyteller holds out hands, letting the child make the decision to hug, hold hands or not touch at all. The storyteller says goodbye and reflects on the pleasure of having the child in this community.

In the research setting, the opening, presentation of the lesson and wondering aloud together about the lesson might take about half an hour. The children's response to the lesson through art, retelling and other work might take about an hour. The preparation for the feast, the feast and saying goodbye might take another half an hour.

IF YOU ONLY HAVE THE FAMOUS 45-MINUTE HOUR

You may have a limited time for your sessions—as little as forty-five minutes instead of two hours. With a forty-five minute session, you have several choices.

FOCUS ON THE FEAST

Sometimes children take especially long to get ready. If you need a full fifteen minutes to build the circle, you can move directly to the feast, leaving time for a leisurely goodbye. You will not shortchange the children. The quality of time and relationships that the children experience within the space is the most important lesson presented in a session of Godly Play.

FOCUS ON THE WORD

Most often, you will have time for a single presentation, including time for the children and you to respond to the lesson by wondering together. Finish with the feast and then the goodbye ritual. Because the children will have no time to make a work response, we suggest that every three or four sessions, you omit any presentation and focus on the work instead (see directly below.)

FOCUS ON THE WORK

If you usually must pass from the presentation directly to the feast, then every three or four sessions, substitute a work session for a presentation. First build the circle, then, without making a presentation, help children choose their work for the day. Allow enough time at the end of the session to share the feast and say goodbye.

HOW TO ADD ENRICHMENT PRESENTATIONS TO YOUR SCHEDULE OF STORIES

The fifteen enrichment presentations in *Godly Play Volume 6* are meant to be integrated into *Godly Play Volume 2*. Introduce these new presentations to the children when they are ready for more. When will that be? Our experience has shown that if children have Godly Play from an early age, they will be ready for more at about age seven, but every child is different and therefore every circle of children is different. Some will be ready sooner than seven and some much later. Whenever you introduce new lessons, it is important that these enrichment stories stay linked to the stories on the "top shelf" in your classroom. Be sure to revisit the stories on the top shelf regularly, even as you introduce the new material in *Volume 6*. You can do this by presenting the top shelf story, or by simply bringing the material to the circle and asking the children what they remember about it. This will help them to place the figures in the enrichment lessons within the core stories, carefully sequenced on the top shelf.

HOW TO MANAGE SPACE

GETTING STARTED

We strongly recommend a thorough reading of *The Complete Guide to Godly Play, Volume 1: How to Lead Godly Play Lessons*.

To start, focus on the relationships and actions that are essential to Godly Play, rather than on the materials needed in a fully equipped Godly Play space. We know that not every parish can allocate generous funds for Christian education. We believe Godly Play is worth beginning with the simplest of resources. Without any materials at all, two teachers can make a Godly Play space that greets the children, shares a feast and blesses them goodbye each week.

When Jerome Berryman began his teaching, he used shelving made from boards and cinder blocks, and only one presentation material: figures for the parable of the Good Shepherd, cut from construction paper and placed in a shoe box he had spray-painted gold.

Over the year, Berryman filled the shelves with additional homemade lesson materials. When more time and money became available, he upgraded those materials to ones cut from foam core. Now his research room is fully equipped with the full range of beautiful and lasting Godly Play materials: parable boxes, Noah's ark, a desert box filled with sand. All of these riches are wonderful gifts to the children who spend time there, but the *start* of a successful Godly Play environment is the nurturing of appropriate relationships in a safe space.

MATERIALS FOR GODLY PLAY, VOLUME 6

MATERIALS NEEDED FOR THE PRESENTATIONS

Each lesson details the materials needed in a section titled "Notes on the Materials." Here is a list of all suggested materials for these fifteen enrichment presentations:

- *Enrichment Lesson 1: Second Creation: "The Falling Apart"*
  — hollow wooden apple containing "differences"
  — 2 fruit trees
  — 2 People of God (Adam and Eve)
  — serpent
  — green felt underlay

- *Enrichment Lesson 2: The Story of Abraham*
  — 3 rocks
  — 3 clear boxes (one filled with sand, one dust, one silver stars)
  — statue of three figures
  — small pieces of wood wrapped in twine
  — bowl of "fire"
  — small knife
  — long piece of twine
  — ram
  — cave
  — tan felt underlay

- *Enrichment Lesson 3: The Story of Sarah*
  — 5 People of God (Sarah, Abraham, Hagar, Ishmael and Isaac)
  — tent
  — 2 baby blankets
  — spring of water
  — sack of grain
  — cave
  — a felt underlay

- *Enrichment Lesson 4: The Story of Jacob*
  — 14 People of God (Jacob, Esau and Jacob's 12 sons)
  — soup bowl
  — fake animal skin
  — ladder & rock
  — 2 wedding veils
  — sign saying *Peniel*
  — tan felt underlay

- *Enrichment Lesson 5: The Story of Joseph*
  — 12 People of God (12 sons of Jacob)
  — coat of many colors
  — 12 heads of grain
  — image of sun, moon, and stars (from "Creation," *Volume 2*, p. 41, Day 4)
  — clear box filled with 20 silver coins
  — pyramid
  — cow
  — ear of corn
  — sack of grain
  — tan felt underlay

- *Enrichment Lesson 6: The Story of Moses*
  — Baby Moses in basket
  — green felt reeds
  — burning bush
  — 2 pieces of "felt water" (the Red Sea)
  — 2 quail
  — "manna" in clear box
  — staff & rock
  — Mount Sinai (from "Ten Best Ways," *Volume 2*, p. 73)
  — golden calf
  — broken Ten Commandment tablets
  — Ark of the Covenant

- *Enrichment Lesson 7: The Story of Ruth*
  - — model of Bethlehem
  - — 9 People of God
  - — stalks of grain
  - — crown
  - — blue yarn to represent the Jordan River
  - — dark brown felt underlay

- *Enrichment Lesson 8: The Story of Samuel*
  - — Ark of the Covenant
  - — baby wrapped in blanket
  - — 3 coats (each slightly larger than the other)
  - — sleeping mat
  - — small clear bottle of oil
  - — crown
  - — dark brown felt underlay

- *Enrichment Lesson 9: The Story of King David*
  - — small clear bottle of oil
  - — harp
  - — 5 smooth stones
  - — sling shot
  - — shepherd's staff
  - — 2 People of God
  - — crown
  - — Ark of the Covenant
  - — small gold Parable Box (contains green underlay 3" x 3", 2 tan felt houses [one smaller than the other], 5 small sheep)
  - — image of Jerusalem
  - — purple felt underlay

- *Enrichment Lesson 10: The Story of the Prophet Elijah*
  - — crown
  - — black raven
  - — grain in small sack
  - — container of oil
  - — 2 wooden altars
  - — 12 stones
  - — Mount Sinai (from "Ten Best Ways," *Volume 2*, p. 73)
  - — painting or icon of Elijah going up in his chariot of fire
  - — dark brown felt underlay

- *Enrichment Lesson 11: The Story of the Prophet Isaiah*
  — wood swirls of color and the words "Holy, Holy, Holy" and music
  — coal (piece of wood painted to resemble burning coal)
  — grapes (plastic)
  — votive candle
  — chain
  — strip of brown felt
  — 1 of the People of God
  — rock
  — beautiful garment
  — statue of mother surrounded by children
  — scroll (like the one in "The Synagogue and the Upper Room," *Volume 4,* p. 99)
  — wolf & sheep (exactly like what is used in the "Parable of the Good Shepherd," *Volume 3*, p. 77)
  — Creation story (from the top shelf, *Volume 2*, p. 41)
  — dark brown felt underlay

- *Enrichment Lesson 12: The Story of the Prophet Jeremiah*
  — shofar
  — lion & a wolf
  — Summary of the Law (from "The Ten Best Ways," *Volume 2*, p. 73)
  — linen belt
  — broken pieces of clay pottery
  — cup filled with "poison"
  — plate of nasty food
  — chain (10 inches long)
  — pyramid
  — image of Jerusalem restored
  — dark brown felt underlay

- *Enrichment Lesson 13: The Story of the Prophet Ezekiel*
  — chain (10 inches long)
  — image of Ezekiel's vision of God (the wheel, etc.)
  — scroll
  — brick
  — Good Shepherd and ordinary Shepherd (just like what is used in the "Parable of the Good Shepherd," *Volume 3*, p. 77)
  — small pitcher
  — collection of "dry bones"
  — image of Jerusalem restored
  — dark brown felt underlay

- *Enrichment Lesson 14: The Story of Daniel*
  — chain (10 inches long)
  — painting of a golden figure mounted on a wooden plaque (Daniel 2:31ff)

- golden statue
- painting of a great tree covered with fruit and surrounded by animals of all kinds mounted on a wooden plaque
- wooden plaque painted to look like a grey stone wall with the words *Mene, Mene, Tekel, Parsin* written in Hebrew on it
- lion's den
- paintings of Daniel's four visions (the four beasts, Daniel 7:1-8; the ram and the he-goat, Daniel 8:1-10; Gabriel, Daniel 9:20-27; the man clothed in linen, Daniel 10:5-7)
- 2-sectioned underlay (dark brown felt for first part; multi-colored cloth for visions)

- *Enrichment Lesson 15: The Story of Job*
  - 2 6" squares of green felt
  - 1 6" square of brown felt
  - 1 6" square of grey felt
  - 12 People of God (Job, Mrs. Job, 3 figures representing Job's 10 children, 3 more figures representing Job's new family; Job's 4 friends)
  - 2 camels
  - 2 sheep
  - 2 cows
  - whirlwind
  - fish hook
  - 10" length of fishing line
  - dark brown felt underlay

MATERIALS FOR CHILDREN'S WORK

Gather art supplies that the children can use to make their responses. These materials are kept on the art shelves. We suggest:
- paper
- painting trays
- watercolor
- paints and brushes
- drawing boards
- crayons, pencils and markers
- boards for modeling clay
- clay rolled into small balls in airtight containers

MATERIALS FOR THE FEAST

- napkins
- serving basket
- cups
- tray
- pitcher

MATERIALS FOR CLEANUP

Gather cleaning materials that the children can use to clean up after their work and use to care for their environment. We suggest:

- paper towels
- feather duster
- brush and dustpan
- cleaning cloths
- spray bottles with water
- trash can with liner.

HOW TO ARRANGE THE MATERIAL ON THE SHELVES

The materials are arranged to communicate visually and silently the language system of the Christian faith: our sacred stories, parables and our liturgical actions. Main presentations (*Godly Play Volumes 2, 3 and 4*) are generally kept on the top shelves.

Enrichment presentations are added to the second and third shelves in classrooms of experienced Godly Players. Each enrichment lesson is identified with its own *story icon.* A story icon is an image that invites the child to wonder about what is in the container that holds the story. Each lesson includes the underlay and the teaching objects for telling the narrative.

In the bottom of each story container is a *control.* A control unfolds to be the full length of the underlay. On each control is an outline of the teaching objects in the proper sequence so the children can check their own work. If you change the sequence, you change the story.

When room permits, supplemental materials can be gathered such as books, maps or other resources. Separate shelves hold supplies for art, cleanup and the feast. A shelf for children's work in progress is also very important.

What follows is a basic map of a Godly Play room. This is a view looking down from the top, highlighting the location of the Old Testament Sacred Story shelves. Within each of the 15 enrichment presentations in this volume, you will find a diagram showing the shelves from the front. This diagram does not show the actual materials or the container in which the material is organized. It is only to show the approximate location under the appropriate core Sacred Story. The location of the materials for each presentation (teaching objects, etc.) is highlighted on the diagram.

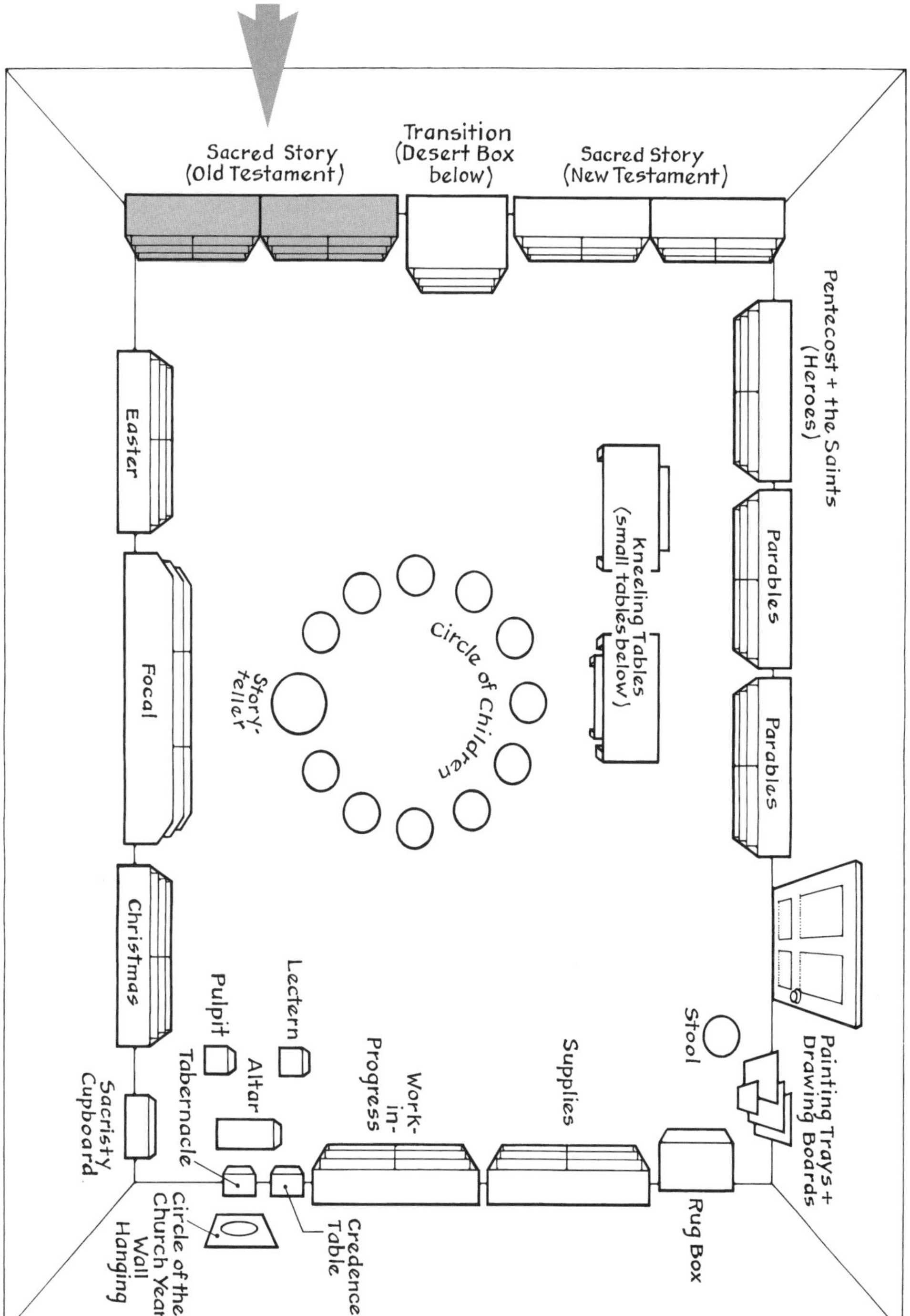
Sacred Story
(Old Testament)
Transition
(Desert Box
below)
Sacred Story
(New Testament)
Pentecost + the Saints
(Heroes)
Parables
Parables
Kneeling Tables
(small tables below)
Easter
Focal
Christmas
Circle of Children
Story-
teller
Lectern
Pulpit
Altar
Tabernacle
Sacristy
Cupboard
Work-
in-
Progress
Supplies
Stool
Painting Trays +
Drawing Boards
Rug Box
Credence
Table
Circle of the
Church Year
Wall
Hanging

WHERE TO FIND MATERIALS (TEACHING OBJECTS)

HOW TO MANAGE RELATIONSHIPS

THE TWO TEACHING ROLES: DOOR PERSON AND STORYTELLER

Each teaching role fosters respect for the children and the Godly Play space. For example, parents are left at the threshold of the Godly Play space and teachers remain at the children's eye level. Both practices keep the room child-centered, instead of adult-centered.

Similarly when the storyteller presents a lesson, he or she keep eye focus on the materials of the lesson—now the children. Instead of being encouraged to respond to a teacher, the children are invited, by the storyteller's eyes, to enter the story.

In a typical Sunday morning session, only two adults will be present in the Godly Play space; the door person and the storyteller. These are their respective tasks during typical session:

DOOR PERSON

Check the shelves, especially the supply shelves and art shelves.

Get out the roll book, review notes and get ready to greet the children and parents.

Slow down the children coming into the room. You may need to take and put aside toys, books and other distracting objects. Help them to get ready. Take the roll or have the older children check themselves in.

Close the door when it is time. Be ready to work with latecomers and children who come to you from the circle.

Avoid casual eye contact with the story-teller to help prevent the adults in the room from turning the children into objects, talking down to them or manipulating them.

When the children choose their work, they may need help setting up artwork and getting materials from the shelves for work on a lesson, either alone or in a group.

STORYTELLER

Check the material to be presented that day.

Get seated on the floor in the circle and prepare to greet the children.

Guide the children to places in the circle where they will best be able to attend to the lesson. Visit quietly until it is time to begin and all are ready.

Present the lesson. Model how to "enter" the material.

Draw the children into the lesson by your introduction. Bring your gaze down to focus on the material when you begin the actual lesson. Look up when the wondering begins.

After the lesson and wondering, go around the circle, dismissing each child to begin his or her work, one at a time. Each child chooses what to do. Go quickly around the circle the first time,

DOOR PERSON

STORYTELLER

returning to the children who did not decide. Go around the circle for decisions until only a few are left. These may be new or for some other reason cannot make a choice. Present a lesson to these children.

Stay in your chair unless children need your help. Do not intrude on the community of children. Stay at the eye level of the children whenever possible, as if there is a glass ceiling in the room at the level of the taller children.

Remain seated in the circle unless children need help with the lessons they have gotten out. You may need to help with art materials. Keep yourself at the children's eye level as you help.

Help the children put their work away, and also help the children who are getting ready to lay out the feast.

When it is time for the feast, go to the light switch and turn it off. Ask the children to put their work away and come back to the circle for the feast. Turn the light back on. Go to the circle to anchor it as the children finish their work and return.

Sit quietly in your chair. Be sure that the trash can has a liner in it.

Ask for prayers, but do not pressure. After the feast, show the children how to put their things away in the trash.

Greet the parents and begin to call the names of the children who are ready and whose parents are there.

Help the children get ready to have their names called.

If a child starts for the door without saying goodbye to the storyteller, remind him or her to return to the storyteller to say goodbye.

As the children's names are called, they come to you. Hold out your hands. Children can take your hands, give a hug or keep their distance, as they like. Tell them quietly and privately how glad you were to see them and what good work they did today. Invite them to come back when they can.

Remember to give back anything that may have been taken at the beginning of class.

Take time to enjoy saying goodbye, with all the warmth of a blessing for each child.

When the children are gone, check and clean the art and supply shelves.

When all are gone, check the material shelves and clean.

DOOR PERSON

Sit quietly and contemplate the session as a whole.

Evaluate, make notes and discuss the session with your co-teacher.

STORYTELLER

Sit quietly and contemplate the session as a whole.

Evaluate, make notes and discuss the session with your co-teacher.

HOW OTHERS CAN HELP

Other adults who want to support the work of a Godly Play space can contribute by:
- taking turns providing festive and healthy food for the children to share during their feasts
- keeping the art and supply shelves replenished with fresh materials
- using their creative skills to make materials for Godly Play presentations.

HOW TO RESPOND EFFECTIVELY TO DISRUPTIONS IN THE CIRCLE

You always want to model the behavior you expect in the circle—focused on the lesson and respectful of everyone in the circle. If a disruption occurs, you deal with that disruption in such a way that you still show continual respect for everyone in the circle—including the child who is having trouble that day. You also still maintain as much focus on the lesson as you can, returning to complete focus on the lesson as quickly as possible.

Therefore, as you consider responses, remember to keep a neutral tone in your voice. Remember, too, that your goal is to help the child move himself or herself toward more appropriate behavior. At the first level of interruption, you might simply raise your eyes from the material. You look up, but not directly at the child, while saying, "We need to get ready again. Watch. This is how we get ready." Model the way to get ready and begin again the presentation where you left off.

If the interruption continues or increases, address the child directly. "No, that's not fair. Look at all these children who are listening. They are ready. You need to be ready, too. Let's try again. Good. That's the way."

If the interruption still continue or increases, ask the child to sit by the door person. Don't think of this as a punishment or as an exclusion from the story: some children *want* to sit by the door person for their own reasons. Continue to keep a neutral tone of voice as you say, "I think you need to sit by (*door person's name*). You can see and hear from there. The lesson is still for you."

The goal is for the child to take himself or herself to the door. If the child is having trouble, or says, "No!", you can say, "May I help you?" Only if necessary do you gently pick up the child or, in some similar way, help him or her go to the door person.

EARLY, MIDDLE AND LATE CHILDHOOD

When we say or write the word *child* or *childhood* something interesting happens. The listener or reader projects a child's image into the ambiguity of our words. These listeners and readers will select from early, middle or late childhood the periods and, perhaps, even particular children from their experience to give "their" meaning to "our" thoughts. So, let's agree that when we talk about children we specify whether we are talking about early, middle or late childhood. Let's further agree that we will give approximate age spans for these three great developmental periods as roughly 3-6, 6-9 and 9-12 years. Each child goes through the great periods at his or her own rate, and psychologists differ on what these age groups might be.

In Godly Play the children in early childhood are mostly interested in how the class works. How do you come into the room? How do you sit in a circle and listen? How do you get the educational materials from the shelf? How do you go and get your art materials? How do you put things away? How do you have a feast? How do you leave the room? These are the sorts of things they are working out. They also learn how to "love" the materials and how to be at play in the wondering with the other children about what the presentations mean. If one has taught, mostly by authentic showing, how to love the language of the Christian People, then something amazing and huge has happened. It is the foundation on which middle and late childhood will be built.

In middle childhood the children who are experienced with Godly Play are now free to work smoothly in the classroom. They know many of the lessons with their senses, even if they cannot yet articulate what they are about with words. A foundation has been laid with their body knowing. In middle childhood the emphasis is on speaking and reading. The reading, however, may still be at the word-reading level and not yet on the paragraph-reading level. Children are still not fully at ease with the printed page. This is why, for example, the Parable Synthesis Lessons (Parable Syntheses 1, Parable Synthesis 2 and Parable Synthesis 3 on pages 132-152 in *Godly Play Volume 3*) are not presented until late childhood; it has too much reading involved. Before children begin to rely on their eyes to understand the language of the Christian People, we like for them to have deep knowledge of this language that is based on their other senses. What is most interesting about middle childhood for Godly Play is that the children's wondering becomes verbally richer.

Children in late childhood require teachers who are very experienced with all of the stories on the shelves. It is not possible to predict what direction they will go in their wondering and work, so a teacher needs to be ready to go just about anywhere with them. This is difficult for an inexperienced teacher. Children in late childhood have also become savvy schoolgoers by this time, and will be more anxious to know what the "correct" answer is. The energy required at this stage to support the children's wondering and ability to find their own answers is sometimes exhausting but important. The goal is to help children to remain open to new ideas but at the same time to be rooted in the Christian tradition.

In late childhood the ability to be at ease with reading paragraphs and books allows the children to take books from the shelves of the Godly Play environment and enjoy reading them. Sometimes, however, this is not to their advantage. Some children will curl up with a book and not be as aware of the community of children swirling around them. They can also use the reading as a defense against emotional involvement with the sacred stories, the parables, the liturgical action materials and sensitivity to God's presence in the silent spaces between words. While an adult guide might want to move children in middle childhood towards reading, in late childhood the guide might want to move the older children back toward the materials so they can once again put their hands on this powerful language.

If you would like to read more about the theological and educational foundations for Godly Play there are concise articles by Jerome W. Berryman in the *Sewanee Theological Review* (Volume 48: Volume 1, Christmas 2004 and Volume 4, Michaelmas 2005).

HOW TO SUPPORT THE CHILDREN'S "WORK" (DEEP PLAY)

Support can be shown in two key ways: by the structure of the classroom and by the language used. Let's explore both of these.

CLASSROOM STRUCTURE

A Godly Play classroom is structured to support children's work in four ways:
- First, it makes materials inviting and available by keeping the room open, clean and well-organized. A useful phrase for a Godly Play room is, "This material is for you. You can touch this and work with this when you want to. If you haven't had the lesson, ask one of the other children or the storyteller to show it to you." Children walking into a Godly Play classroom take delight at all the fascinating materials calling out to them. These materials say, "This room is for you."
- Second, it encourages responsible stewardship of the shared materials by helping children learn to take care of the room themselves. When something is spilled, we could quickly wipe it up ourselves, of course. Instead, by helping children learn to take care of their own spills, we communicate to them the respect we have for their own problem-solving capabilities. At the end of work time, each child learns to put away materials carefully. In fact, some children may want to choose cleaning work—dusting or watering plants—for their response time.
- Third, it provides a respectful place for children's work by reserving space in the room for ongoing or finished projects. When a child is still working on a project at the end of work time, reassure him or her by saying, "This project will be here for you next week. You can take as many weeks as you need to finish it. We never lose work in a Godly Play room." Sometimes children want to give a finished piece of work to the room. Sometimes children want to take either finished or unfinished work home. These choices are theirs to make and ours to respect.
- Fourth, it sets a leisurely pace that allows children to engage deeply in their chosen responses. This is why, when we are pressed for time, it's better to do no more than

build the circle, share a feast and lovingly say goodbye rather than rush through a story and time of art response. When we tell a story, we want to allow enough time for leisurely wondering together. When we provide work time, we want to allow enough time for children to become deeply engaged in their work.

In their wondering or their work, children may be dealing with deep issues—issues that matter as much as life and death. Provide them a nourishing *space* filled with safe time for this deep work.

USING LANGUAGE

You can also support children with the language you use:

- Choose *"open" responses*. We choose "open" responses when we simply describe what we see, rather than evaluate the children or their work. Open responses invite children's interaction, but respect children's choices to simply keep working in silence, too. *Examples:*
  — Hmm. Lots of red.
  — This is big work. The paint goes all the way from here to there.
  — This clay looks so smooth and thin now.
- Avoid *evaluative responses*. Evaluative responses shift the child's focus from his or her work to your praise. In a Godly Play classroom, we want to allow children the freedom to work on what matters most to them, not for the reward of our praise. *Examples to avoid*:
  — You're a wonderful painter.
  — This is a great picture.
  — I'm so please with what you did.
- Choose *empowering responses*, which emphasize each child's ability to make choices, solve problems and articulate needs. In a Godly Play classroom, a frequently heard phrase is *That's the way; you can do this.* We encourage children to choose their own work, get the materials out carefully and clean up their work areas when they are done. When a child spills something, respond with *That's no problem. Do you know where the clean-up supplies are kept?* If a child needs help, show where the supplies are kept or how to wring out a sponge. When helping, the aim is to restore ownership of the problem or situation to the child as soon as possible.
- Stay alert to the children's needs during work and cleanup. The Door Person's role is especially important as children get out and put away their work. By staying alert to the children's choices in the circle, the Door Person can know when to help a new child learn the routine for using clay, when a child might need help moving the desert box, or when a child might need support in putting material away or cleaning up after painting.

MORE INFORMATION ON GODLY PLAY

The Complete Guide to Godly Play, Volumes 1-8 by Jerome Berryman are available from Morehouse Education Resources. *Volume 1: How to Lead Godly Play Lessons* is the essential handbook for using Godly Play in church school or a wide variety of alternative settings. *Volumes 2-4* present complete presentations for Fall, Winter and Spring. *Volumes 6-8* contain a series of enrichment lessons to be integrated with *Volumes 2, 3, and 4. Volume 5* includes the wisdom of Godly Play trainers.

The *Godly Play Foundation* is the nonprofit organization that sponsors ongoing research, training, development of materials, accreditation programs, the development of a theology of childhood, and supports high-quality Godly Play practice around the world.

The *Godly Play Foundation* is an ecumenical and parish-based organization with centers of excellence in this country and around the world. For locations of these centers please visit our Web site at *www.godlyplay.org*

The *Foundation* maintains a schedule of training and speaking events related to Godly Play, and a list of trainers available throughout this and other countries for help in establishing Godly Play programs. For more information, contact:

Godly Play Foundation
Physical address: 1551 10 Ave. E, Seattle, WA 98102
Mailing address: P.O. Box 23320, Seattle, WA 98102
Phone: 206-619-3145
www.godlyplay.org
center@godlyplay.org

Although you can make your own materials, Morehouse Education Resources now supplies the beautiful and lasting materials approved by the *Godly Play Foundation* especially for use in a Godly Play classroom. For more information or to place an order, contact:

Morehouse Education Resources
4775 Linglestown Road
Harrisburg, PA 17112
1-800-242-1918
fax: 1-717-541-8136
www.morehouseeducation.org

SECOND CREATION: "THE FALLING APART"

LESSON NOTES

FOCUS: "THE FALLING APART" AND COMING BACK TOGETHER IN A NEW WAY (GENESIS 2:4–3:24)

- SACRED STORY
- ENRICHMENT LESSON

THE MATERIAL

- LOCATION: OLD TESTAMENT SACRED STORY SHELVES, MIDDLE SHELF, UNDER "CREATION"
- PIECES: HOLLOW WOODEN APPLE CONTAINING "DIFFERENCES," 2 TREES, ADAM, EVE, SERPENT
- UNDERLAY: GREEN FELT

BACKGROUND

The key people whose stories are told in this volume enrich and extend the core narrative (*Volume 2*), which tells how the People of God sought the elusive presence of God. In *Volume 2* we began at the beginning with the first creation story. Here we also begin at the beginning with *Adam-Eve* and how they "fell apart" from God, from each other, from God's creation, and from the image of God in their deep selves. We learn how these relationships were restored.

NOTES ON THE MATERIAL

The material is placed in a deep-sided wicker or wooden tray (12" x 8" x 3"). The story icon (5" x 2.5") is an image of Adam and Eve. It can be attached to the end or the side of the tray depending on the size of the shelves, the classroom or other considerations. The underlay is a piece of green felt, approximately 18" square with slightly rounded corners. It is folded to fit in the tray. In addition you will need two wooden fruit trees, figures for Adam and Eve, a wooden serpent, a hollow wooden apple containing the "differences." The differences are mounted on card stock or to make them more permanent on small, thin pieces of wood.

SPECIAL NOTES

The core stories about the People of God are placed on the top of the sacred story shelves. The enrichment stories about the key people in the core stories are placed on the lower shelves of the sacred story section in the room, under the core stories they enrich and extend (see diagram below).

When you introduce the stories in this volume, take care to set them in the larger context of the sacred story of which they are a part. You can accomplish this by:
- presenting the top shelf story the week before and then following up with this,
- presenting the top shelf story briefly on the same day you present this, or
- standing by the shelf and reminding the children of the top shelf story before bringing this one to the circle.

STORY ICON FOR SECOND CREATION: "THE FALLING APART"

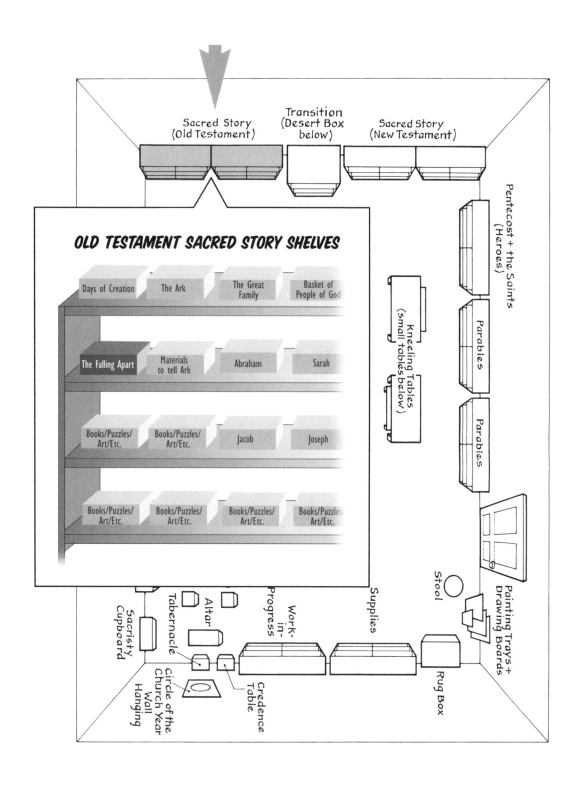

OLD TESTAMENT SACRED STORY SHELVES

Sacred Story (Old Testament)

Transition (Desert Box below)

Sacred Story (New Testament)

Days of Creation	The Ark	The Great Family	Basket of People of God
The Falling Apart	Materials to tell Ark	Abraham	Sarah
Books/Puzzles/Art/Etc.	Books/Puzzles/Art/Etc.	Jacob	Joseph
Books/Puzzles/Art/Etc.	Books/Puzzles/Art/Etc.	Books/Puzzles/Art/Etc.	Books/Puzzles/Art/Etc.

Kneeling Tables (small tables below)

Pentecost + the Saints (Heroes)

Parables

Parables

Stool

Painting Trays + Drawing Boards

Supplies

Work-in-Progress

Rug Box

Sacristy Cupboard

Tabernacle

Altar

Circle of the Church Year Wall Hanging

Credence Table

WHERE TO FIND MATERIALS (TEACHING OBJECTS)

MOVEMENTS	WORDS
Move with deliberation to the shelf where the material waits.	Watch. Watch where I go.
Pick up the tray containing the material and return to the circle. You may need to say:	Everyone needs to be ready.
Spread out the underlay in front of you. Lower your hand onto the underlay as you say, "It is good," like a blessing—just like you do when you tell story of the first creation (Volume 2, p. 41) and "bless" each day.	When God created everything, God said, "It is good." And God put God's own image in the creatures that walk on the earth. In the midst of the creation there was a wonderful garden. It was God's garden. Everything was there, but everything was so close it was all together. God was with the rocks and plants and animals, and they were with God and each other. All the people were also together in one person who was called "Everyone" or, in their language, "Adam."
Place the figures for Adam and Eve on the underlay so that they are physically touching, as if they are one person (Adam/Eve).	

ADAM AND EVE AS ADAM-EVE (STORYTELLER'S PERSPECTIVE)

MOVEMENTS	WORDS
	Eve was there too. She was always there, for she came from Adam. She and Adam were a kind of *Adam-Eve.*
Place the two trees behind Adam-Eve.	In the middle of the garden grew two trees. God told *Adam-Eve* that they should not eat the fruit from these trees. One tree was about *differences* and one tree was about *forever.* If you ate the fruit of the tree of differences, you would know about differences, and if you ate from the forever tree, you would live forever.

MOVEMENTS	WORDS

MOVEMENTS

Put the serpent beside Adam-Eve.

Separate Adam-Eve so they are now Adam and Eve.

WORDS

Now, the serpent was more clever than any other creature that the Lord God made. And he suggested that *Adam-Eve* taste the fruit from the tree of differences. And they did.

Adam-Eve ate from the tree of differences and things fell apart for them. They became Adam *and* Eve. The difference between them and God also came apart. And the difference between good and evil did too.

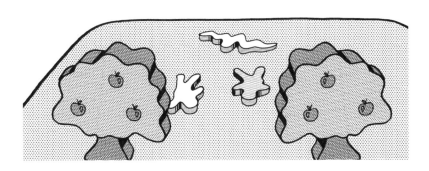

ADAM AND EVE AFTER EATING FROM TREE OF DIFFERENCES (STORYTELLER'S PERSPECTIVE)

Cover Adam and Eve with your hand when you say that they hid. Uncover them when you say that God found them.

God called for them and they hid, but God found them. They did not know how to be with God anymore, because of all the differences.

Pick up the wooden apple and open the lid. Pull out the "differences" and place them on the underlay beside the figures—good and evil, close and far, high and low, God and people, Adam and Eve.

There were: good and evil, close and far, high and low, God and people, Adam and Eve...and many more.

MOVEMENTS	WORDS

THE MANY DIFFERENCES (CHILDREN'S PERSPECTIVE)

The differences also did something wonderful. Now Adam and Eve could take things apart and put them back together again. They could be creators, almost like God. They couldn't make something out of nothing, but they could make something out of differences.

After the differences, Adam and Eve could not go back to when everything was all together in the Garden. They could only go forward and they did.

Push Adam and Eve to the edge of the garden and place your hand at their backs when you speak of the sword and the angel.

God sent Adam and Eve out of the Garden. An angel and a sword was put at the edge of the Garden so they could not go back, but only go forward. God went with them on their journey to help them be the best creators they could be, and to be with God in this new way, and to stay one with God.

MOVEMENTS

Sit for a moment and look at the story to let the story rest. Then begin the wondering.

After the wondering is over, put the story away carefully. Name each item, saying for example, "Here is the tree of differences. And here is the tree of forever." After all of the story is back in the tray, carefully model how to fold the underlay and place it in the tray as well. Return the lesson to its place on the shelf. Then return to your spot in the circle and dismiss the children one by one to their work.

WORDS

I wonder what part of this story you liked the best?

I wonder what part was the most important?

I wonder what part of the story was about you, or what part you were in?

I wonder if we can leave out any of the story and still have all that we need?

ENRICHMENT LESSON 2
THE STORY OF ABRAHAM

LESSON NOTES
FOCUS: THE FATHER OF THE GREAT FAMILY (GENESIS 12:24–25:11)
- SACRED STORY
- ENRICHMENT PRESENTATION

THE MATERIAL
- LOCATION: OLD TESTAMENT SACRED STORY SHELVES, MIDDLE SHELF, UNDER "THE GREAT FAMILY"
- PIECES: ROCKS FOR ALTARS (THREE), 3 CLEAR BOXES (ONE WITH SAND, ONE DUST, ONE STARS), STATUE OF 3 STRANGERS, WOOD FOR THE OFFERING WRAPPED IN TWINE, BOWL OF FIRE, KNIFE, LONG PIECE OF TWINE, RAM, CAVE
- CONTROL
- UNDERLAY: TAN FELT STRIP, 42" X 11"

BACKGROUND

"The Great Family" has become as many as the stars in the sky and the grains of sand in the desert. But there is still an original mother and a father to remember, honor and learn from. This story enriches the story of "the Great Family" (*Volume 2*, p. 57) by telling more about Abraham, the father of "the Great Family." It includes how God tested Abraham and Abraham tested God.

NOTES ON THE MATERIAL

Abraham's story sits in a deep wooden or wicker tray (12" x 8" x 3"). The story icon (5" x 2.5") is a drawing of Abraham looking out at the stars. It can be attached to the end or the side of the tray depending on the size of the shelves, the classroom or other considerations. The underlay is a strip of tan felt, 42" x 11". Each object in the story is approximately the same size (no more than 4" high and 4" wide). The story calls for the following objects: three rocks to remind the children of the three places in the desert where Abraham came close to God; three clear boxes (one filled with sand, one dust, and one stars), a statue of the three strangers, wood for the offering wrapped in twine, a bowl of fire (a small clay bowl with clay painted red on the inside to represent the fire), a long piece of twine, a ram and a cave.

A control for the lesson is folded and placed in the tray for the children to use to check their work. The sequence of the story is important because when you change the sequence, you change the story.

SPECIAL NOTES

The core stories about the People of God are placed on the top of the sacred story shelves. The enrichment stories about the key people in the core stories are placed on the lower shelves of the sacred story section in the room, under the core stories they enrich and extend (see diagram below).

Abraham's story enriches the lesson on "The Great Family" (*Volume 2*, p. 57). When you introduce the stories in this volume, take care to set them in the larger context of the sacred story of which they are a part. You can accomplish this by:
• presenting the top shelf story the week before and then following up with this,
• presenting the top shelf story briefly on the same day you present this, or
• standing by the shelf and reminding the children of the top shelf story before bringing this one to the circle.

As you tell the story of Abraham's life, place objects on the underlay to remind you of each important event. Unroll the underlay slowly, providing just enough space for the next object, as if you are unrolling a life.

At the end of the wondering, show the children the control card and then carefully place each object back in the tray saying something about each event like, "Here is the knife for the sacrifice," and so forth. Lastly, model how to roll the underlay back up and place it in the tray.

STORY ICON FOR THE STORY OF ABRAHAM

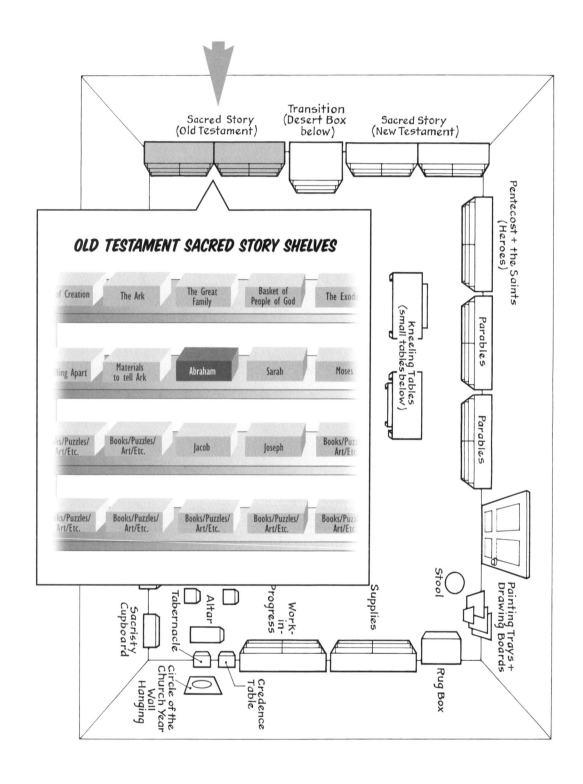

OLD TESTAMENT SACRED STORY SHELVES

Sacred Story (Old Testament)

Transition (Desert Box below)

Sacred Story (New Testament)

Pentecost + the Saints (Heroes)

Parables

Parables

of Creation | The Ark | The Great Family | Basket of People of God | The Exodus

fling Apart | Materials to tell Ark | Abraham | Sarah | Moses

Books/Puzzles/Art/Etc. | Books/Puzzles/Art/Etc. | Jacob | Joseph | Books/Puzzles/Art/Etc.

Books/Puzzles/Art/Etc. | Books/Puzzles/Art/Etc. | Books/Puzzles/Art/Etc. | Books/Puzzles/Art/Etc. | Books/Puzzles/Art/Etc.

Kneeling Tables (small tables below)

Sacristy Cupboard

Tabernacle

Altar

Work-in-Progress

Supplies

Stool

Painting Trays + Drawing Boards

Circle of the Church Year Wall Hanging

Credence Table

Rug Box

WHERE TO FIND MATERIALS (TEACHING OBJECTS)

MOVEMENTS	WORDS
Move with deliberation to the shelf where the material waits.	Watch. Watch where I go.
Pick up Abraham's tray and return to the circle.	
As you return to the circle you may need to say...	We need to be ready.
Take the underlay from the tray and begin to unroll it—just enough to place the first object—right to left (storyteller's perspective).	This is the story of Abraham, the father of the Great Family. He and Sarah went from Ur to Haran and then on into a new land.
*Place **Object #1** (the three rocks representing the altars at Shechem, Bethel and Hebron) on the underlay as you say "God was there" in each place.*	And when they came into the new land, Abraham went up on a hill at Shechem to pray and God was there. He prayed to God at Bethel, and God was there. Then they pitched their tents in Hebron, and God was there too.
*Place **Object #2** (three clear boxes containing sand, stars and dust) on the underlay as you say what each box represents.*	God promised Abraham and Sarah that they would be the mother and father of a great family. The family would be as many as there are grains of sand in the desert, stars in the sky and dust in the land. But Abraham and Sarah had no children
*Place **Object #3** (statue of three strangers]) on the underlay.*	Then three strangers came out of the desert and told them that they would have a child. They laughed. The child was born. And they named him "laughter."
*Place **Object #4** (wood for the offering wrapped in twine) on the underlay.*	Isaac grew. And when he was a boy, God appeared to Abraham and said, "Take your son, your only son, Isaac whom you love, and go to the land of Moriah. Offer him as a burnt offering upon the mountain." The next day he cut the wood and took a donkey, two helpers and his son, and began to walk towards the mountain. On the third day they could see it.
*Place **Object #5** (bowl of fire and a knife) on the underlay.*	Abraham told his helpers to stay there with the donkey, and he and Isaac went on alone. Isaac carried the wood for the offering. And Abraham carried a bowl of fire and the knife.

MOVEMENTS	WORDS

Isaac said, "Here is the fire and the wood, but where is the lamb for the offering?" Abraham said, "God will provide."

*Wrap **Object #6** (piece of twine) around your fingers as you talk about tying up Isaac. Place the twine and the knife on the underlay.*

When they came to the place for the sacrifice, Abraham tied up Isaac. He picked up the knife and was about to kill him for the sacrifice when an Angel came and said, "No. You do not need to do this."

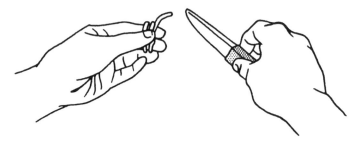

TWINE WRAPPED AROUND FINGERS (STORYTELLER'S PERSPECTIVE)

*Place **Object #7** (ram) on the underlay when you speak of the ram appearing.*

Then Abraham looked, and there was a ram caught in the bushes. God provided the ram for the sacrifice.

Abraham untied Isaac and they went down the mountain. The angel called to him again and said, "God says, 'I will make you the father of a great family…as many as the grains of sand in the desert and the stars in the sky. And I will make of you a great blessing, because you obeyed me.'"

MOVEMENTS	WORDS
Place **Object #8** (cave) on the underlay.	Then Sarah, Abraham's beloved wife, died, and he buried her in a cave at the end of the field near the Oaks of Mamre. After Abraham helped find a wife for Isaac, he died, and was buried in the cave beside Sarah. Isaac and his wife Rebekah had twins, Esau and Jacob, so the Great Family grew.
Sit for a moment and look at the lesson from beginning to end to let the story rest. Then begin the wondering.	I wonder what part of this story you liked the best? I wonder what part of this story was the most important? I wonder what part was about you or what part you were in? I wonder if we could leave any of the story out and still have all that we need?
After the wondering is over, show the children the control card for them to use to check their own telling of the story. Then put the story away carefully. Pick up each object in reverse order and remind the children what the object is, saying for example, "Here is the cave where Abraham and his wife Sarah were buried." After all of the objects are back in the tray, carefully model how to roll the underlay back up and place it in the tray as well. Return the lesson to its place on the shelf. Then return to your spot in the circle and dismiss the children one by one to their work.	

FINAL LAYOUT OF THE STORY OF ABRAHAM (CHILDREN'S PERSPECTIVE)

THE STORY OF SARAH

LESSON NOTES

FOCUS: THE MOTHER OF THE GREAT FAMILY (GENESIS 12–23)

- SACRED STORY
- ENRICHMENT PRESENTATION

THE MATERIAL

- LOCATION: OLD TESTAMENT SACRED STORY SHELVES, MIDDLE SHELF, UNDER "PEOPLE OF GOD"
- PIECES: 2 PEOPLE OF GOD REPRESENTING ABRAHAM AND SARAH, A TENT, BABY BLANKET, A SPRING OF WATER, 3 OF THE PEOPLE OF GOD REPRESENTING HAGAR, ISHMAEL AND ISAAC, A SACK OF GRAIN, A CAVE
- CONTROL
- UNDERLAY: TAN FELT STRIP, 42" X 11"

BACKGROUND

"The Great Family" has become as many as the stars in the sky and the grains of sand in the desert. But there is still an original mother and a father to remember, honor and learn from. This story enriches the story of the "the Great Family" (*Volume 2*, p. 57) by telling more about Sarah, the mother of "the Great Family." It includes the important and complicated relationship between Hagar, Sarah, Abraham, and God.

NOTES ON THE MATERIAL

Sarah's story sits on a deep wooden or wicker tray (12" x 8" x 3"). The story icon (5" x 2.5") is a drawing of Sarah holding Isaac. It can be attached to the end or the side of the tray depending on the size of the shelves, the classroom or other considerations. The underlay is a strip of tan felt, 42" x 11". Each object in the story is approximately the same size (no more than 4" high and 4" wide). The story calls for the following objects: two People of God representing Abraham and Sarah, a tent, two baby blankets, a spring of water, three more of the People of God to represent Hagar, Ishmael and Isaac, a sack of grain and a cave.

A control for the lesson is folded and placed in the tray for the children to use to check their work. The sequence of the story is important because when you change the sequence, you change the story.

SPECIAL NOTES

The core stories about the People of God are placed on the top of the sacred story shelves. The enrichment stories about the key people in the core stories are placed on the lower shelves of the sacred story section in the room, under the core stories they enrich and extend (see diagram below).

Sarah's story enriches the lesson about "the Great Family" (*Volume 2*, p. 57). When you introduce the stories in this volume take care to set them in the larger context of the sacred story of which they are a part. You can accomplish this by:
- presenting the top shelf story the week before and then following up with this,
- presenting the top shelf story briefly on the same day you present this, or
- standing by the shelf and reminding the children of the top shelf story before bringing this one to the circle.

As you tell the story of Sarah's life place objects on the underlay to remind you of each important event. Unroll the underlay slowly, just enough for each object, as if you are unrolling a life. At the end of the wondering, show the children the control card and then carefully place each object back in the tray saying something about each event like, "Here are the three strangers who came out of the desert to tell Sarah that she would have a baby," and so forth. Lastly, model how to roll the underlay back up and place it in the tray.

STORY ICON FOR THE STORY OF SARAH

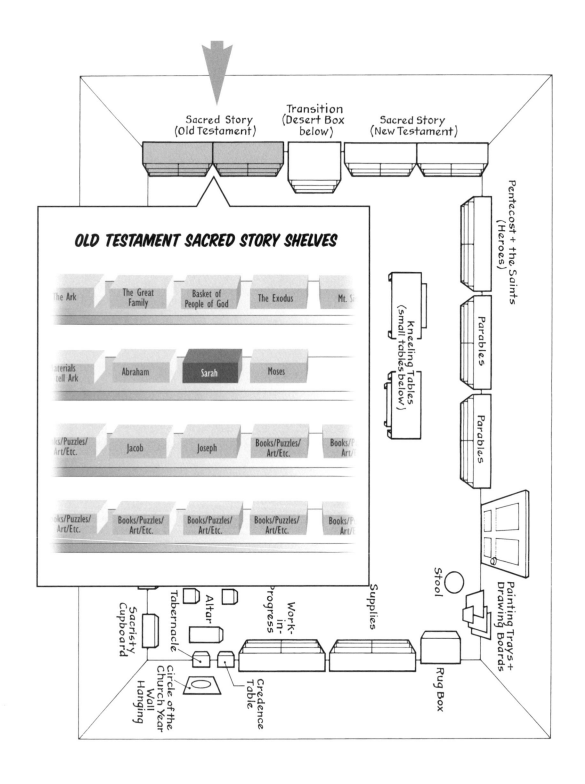

OLD TESTAMENT SACRED STORY SHELVES

Sacred Story (Old Testament)

Transition (Desert Box below)

Sacred Story (New Testament)

The Ark | The Great Family | Basket of People of God | The Exodus | Mt. S...

...aterials ...tell Ark | Abraham | Sarah | Moses

...ks/Puzzles/ Art/Etc. | Jacob | Joseph | Books/Puzzles/ Art/Etc. | Books/P... Art/E...

...oks/Puzzles/ Art/Etc. | Books/Puzzles/ Art/Etc. | Books/Puzzles/ Art/Etc. | Books/Puzzles/ Art/Etc. | Books/P... Art/E...

Pentecost + the Saints (Heroes)

Parables

Parables

Kneeling Tables (small tables below)

Stool

Painting Trays + Drawing Boards

Sacristy Cupboard

Tabernacle

Altar

Work-in-Progress

Supplies

Circle of the Church Year Wall Hanging

Credence Table

Rug Box

WHERE TO FIND MATERIALS (TEACHING OBJECTS)

MOVEMENTS	WORDS
Move with deliberation to the shelf where the material waits.	➤ Watch. Watch where I go.
Pick up the tray containing the material and return to the circle. You may need to say:	➤ Everyone needs to be ready.
Remove the underlay from the tray and unroll it just enough so that the first object will fit, right to left (storyteller's perspective).	
*Place **Object #1** (two People of God like Adam and Eve) on the underlay a little apart. When you say that they "fell in love" push them together.*	➤ Once in the great city of Ur there was a girl named *Sarai*, which means "princess." In the same city there was a man named Abram. They met and fell in love.

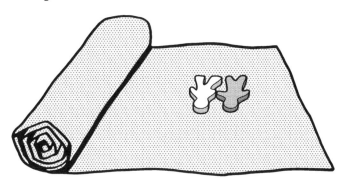

PEOPLE PUSHED TOGETHER (STORYTELLER'S PERSPECTIVE)

*Place **Object #2** (tent) on the underlay.*	➤ They traveled to many new places. God showed them the way. All their lives they lived in tents.
	Sarai was beautiful, even when she was very old. Once they went to Egypt, and the King of Egypt, called the Pharaoh, wanted her for himself. When he discovered that she was Abram's wife he made both of them leave. They went back to the land of Canaan—to Hebron—where they pitched their tent for the last time.
*Place **Object #3** (baby blanket...but no baby) on the underlay.*	➤ Abram and Sarai had been married for a long time, but they had no children. God had promised them that they would be the mother and the father of a great family, but how could that be with no children? This made Sarai worry.
*Place **Object #4** (figure for Hagar) on the underlay.*	➤ Finally, she told Abram to take a second wife, which was a custom in those days. Abram took Hagar, Sarai's helper, for a second wife.

MOVEMENTS

WORDS

When Hagar was about to have a baby, Sarai became angry because *she* wanted to be the mother. Hagar was afraid so she ran away into the wilderness.

*Place **Object #5** (spring of water) on the underlay.*

*Place **Object #6** (figure wrapped in a baby blanket) on the underlay.*

The angel of the Lord found Hagar by a spring of water in the desert and told her to go back. The angel told Hagar that she would have a son and should name him *Ishmael*. She went back and Ishmael was born.

Many years went by and God appeared to Abram. God said to him, "We will be together forever." God also blessed Sarai and promised to give her a son of her own. So Abram became Abraham and Sarai became Sarah.

*Pick up the baby blanket on the underlay and wrap **Object #7** (Isaac) in it when you speak of Isaac's birth. Place it on the underlay next to Ishmael.*

Three strangers came out of the desert. The strangers said, "In the spring of the year God will bless Sarah, and she will have a son." Abraham laughed. Sarah who was standing by the door laughed too, because she was too old.

The strangers heard and said, "Sarah, did you laugh?" She said, "No." She was afraid for some reason.

Sarah did have a son. She named him Isaac, which means laughter.

*Place **Object #8** (sack) on the underlay as you mention the bread and water.*

Sometime later Sarah saw Ishmael, Hagar's son, playing with Isaac. She grew angry all over again, and told Abraham to send them away.

The next morning Abraham gave Hagar and Ishmael some bread and water and sent them into the desert. When they had nothing left to eat or drink, Hagar put Ishmael under a bush and walked far away so she wouldn't have to watch him die. The baby began to cry, and God heard him. An angel came to Hagar and told her to open her eyes. When she did, she saw a well of water. Hagar and Ishmael drank the water and lived. Their family is still alive today.

Take Sarah and Abraham from their positions at the beginning of the lesson and Isaac out of the baby blanket and place them on the underlay beside the sack of food. Take Abraham and Sarah away when you speak of them going away, and then bring them back when you speak of them coming back.

One day Sarah watched Abraham and Isaac go away. They were going to Mt. Moriah. She watched from inside the tent as they left. And the next day she watched for them again...and the next. A week passed. She wondered if she would ever see Isaac again. Finally she saw them coming back and went out to greet them. It was good to have them home again.

MOVEMENTS	WORDS
Place **Object #9** *(cave) on the underlay.*	Then Sarah, full of many years, died. And Abraham buried her in a cave at the end of his new field by the trees. Isaac married *Rebecca*, and they had twins, and "the Great Family" began to grow.
Sit for a moment and look at the lesson from beginning to end to let the story rest. Then begin the wondering.	I wonder what part of this story you liked the best? I wonder what part of this story is the most important? I wonder what part is about you, or is especially for you? I wonder if we can leave out any of the story and still have all that we need?
After the wondering is over, show the children the control card for them to use to check their own telling of the story. Then put the story away carefully. Pick up each object in reverse order and remind the children what the object is, saying for example, "Here is the cave where Sarah was buried." After all of the objects are back in the tray, carefully model how to roll the underlay back up and place it in the tray as well. Return the lesson to its place on the shelf. Then return to your spot in the circle and dismiss the children one by one to their work.	

FINAL LAYOUT FOR THE STORY OF SARAH (CHILDREN'S PERSPECTIVE)

LESSON 4

THE STORY OF JACOB

LESSON NOTES

FOCUS: THE PERSON WHO BECAME ISRAEL (GENESIS 25:19–33:20; 35:16–29)

- SACRED STORY
- ENRICHMENT PRESENTATION

THE MATERIAL

- LOCATION: OLD TESTAMENT SACRED STORY SHELVES, BOTTOM SHELF, UNDER "ABRAHAM"
- PIECES: BASKET WITH 14 PEOPLE OF GOD (JACOB, ESAU AND JACOB'S 12 SONS), SOUP BOWL, FAKE ANIMAL SKIN, LADDER AND ROCK, 2 WEDDING VEILS, WOODEN SIGN SAYING PENIEL
- CONTROL
- UNDERLAY: TAN FELT STRIP, 42" X 11"

BACKGROUND

The story of Jacob adds to the core narrative of the journey of the people of God from the beginning of "the Great Family" to the Exodus.

Isaac and Rebecca had twins, Esau and Jacob. Much of Jacob's story is in his two names. "Jacob" refers to how he was born second and grabbed his brother's heal, but it also means he took his brother's place by trickery (Genesis 25:26). He also wrestled all night with an angel by the Jabok River. The angel named him *Israel* (Genesis 32:28), saying, "for you have striven with God and with man and have prevailed." "Israel" means "one who struggles with God." This is the story about the origin of the twelve tribes of Israel.

NOTES ON THE MATERIAL

Jacob's story sits in a deep wooden or wicker tray (12" x 8" x 3"). The story icon (5" x 2.5") is a drawing of Jacob wrestling with an angel. It can be attached to the end or the side of the tray depending on the size of the shelves, the classroom or other considerations. The underlay is a strip of tan felt, 42" x 11". Each object in the story is approximately the same size (no more than 4" high and 4" wide). The story calls for the following objects: a small basket containing fourteen People of God (Jacob, Esau, and Jacob's twelve sons), a small soup bowl, a piece of fake animal skin, a ladder standing up, a rock with the word *Bethel* written on it, two wedding veils (one for Leah and one for Rachel), piece of wood (3" x 2") with the word *Peniel* written along the bottom of it.

A control for the lesson is folded and placed in the tray for the children to use to check their work. The sequence of the story is important because when you change the sequence, you change the story.

SPECIAL NOTES

The core stories about the People of God are placed on the top of the sacred story shelves. The enrichment stories about the key people in the core stories are placed on the lower shelves of the sacred story section in the room, under the core stories they enrich and extend (see diagram below).

Jacob's story adds to the core narrative the journey of the people of God from the beginning of the Great Family to the Exodus. When you introduce the stories in this volume take care to set them in the larger context of the sacred story of which they are a part.

As you tell the story of Jacob's life, place objects on the underlay to remind you of each important event. Unroll the underlay slowly, just enough for each object, as if you are unrolling a life. At the end of the wondering, show the children the control card and then carefully place each object back in the tray saying something about each event like, "Here are the twelve sons of Jacob," and so forth. Lastly, model how to roll the underlay back up and place it in the tray.

STORY ICON FOR THE STORY OF JACOB

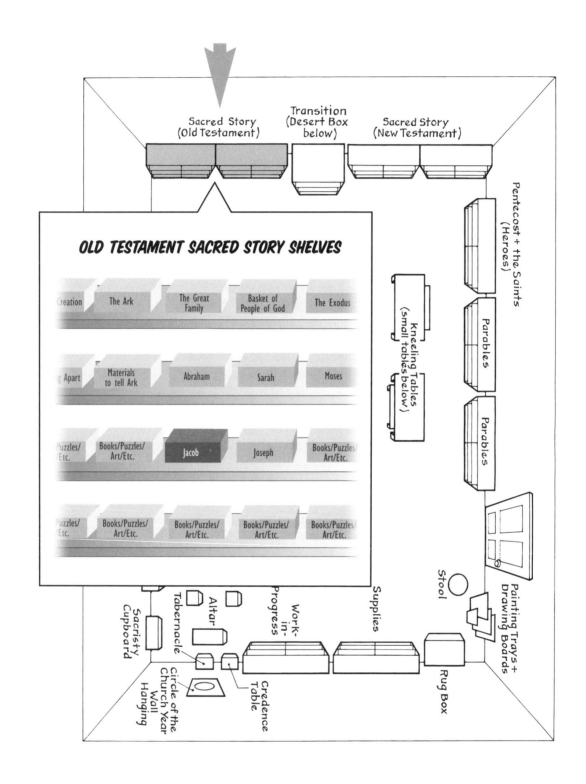

Sacred Story (Old Testament)

Transition (Desert Box below)

Sacred Story (New Testament)

Pentecost + the Saints (Heroes)

Parables

Parables

OLD TESTAMENT SACRED STORY SHELVES

Creation	The Ark	The Great Family	Basket of People of God	The Exodus
g Apart	Materials to tell Ark	Abraham	Sarah	Moses
Puzzles/ Etc.	Books/Puzzles/ Art/Etc.	Jacob	Joseph	Books/Puzzles/ Art/Etc.
Puzzles/ Etc.	Books/Puzzles/ Art/Etc.	Books/Puzzles/ Art/Etc.	Books/Puzzles/ Art/Etc.	Books/Puzzles/ Art/Etc.

Kneeling Tables (small tables below)

Stool

Painting Trays + Drawing Boards

Sacristy Cupboard

Tabernacle

Altar

Work-in-Progress

Supplies

Rug Box

Circle of the Church Year Wall Hanging

Credence Table

WHERE TO FIND MATERIALS (TEACHING OBJECTS)

MOVEMENTS	WORDS
Move with deliberation to the shelf where the material waits.	Watch. Watch where I go.
Pick up the tray containing the material and return to the circle.	
You may need to say:	Everyone needs to be ready.
Remove the underlay from the tray and unroll it so that the first object will fit, right to left (storyteller's perspective).	God promised Abraham that he would be the father of a great family. But Abraham and Sarah had only one son, Isaac.
*Place **Object #1** (two People of God) on the underlay as you mention the twins, Esau and Jacob.*	Isaac married Rebekah. For a long time, they had no children, until with God's help they had two boys, Esau and Jacob.

Esau and Jacob were twins, but they were not like each other. Esau was big and Jacob was small. Esau had red hair and Jacob had dark hair. Esau was hairy and Jacob had smooth skin. Esau liked to hunt and Jacob stayed by the tent to watch the sheep. Esau was born first, so he was the one who was supposed to have his father's things when he died. Isaac loved Esau best but Rebekah loved Jacob best. |
| *Place **Object #2** (soup bowl) on the underlay as you mention the soup.* | Jacob thought it was not fair that Esau was treated special because he was the oldest. They had been born on the same day! Once Esau came home from hunting and he was very hungry. Jacob had made some soup. Esau asked his brother for some. "I will give it to you," said Jacob, "if you will agree that I can have father's things when he dies." Esau did not even think about it. "What use are father's things when I am so hungry?" He took the soup. Now there was an agreement between the brothers that Jacob would be like the oldest son. |
| *Place **Object #3** (animal skin—a piece of fake fur) on the underlay when you mention the animal skins.* | Isaac was old. He could not see. He asked Esau to go hunting and make the stew he liked best. Then Isaac would bless him.

Rebekah overheard this. She thought Jacob should get the blessing. So she and Jacob made Isaac's special stew from a lamb, instead of a wild animal. They put animal skins on Jacob's arms so he would seem hairy and dressed him up like Esau. Jacob went to his father with the stew. Isaac believed that Jacob was Esau and he laid his hands on him and blessed him. |

MOVEMENTS

*Place **Object #4** (rock and ladder) on the underlay as you mention them. Put the rock down with the blank side up; you will turn it over when you speak of the naming of this place.*

Make a pouring motion with your hand to show the pouring of oil. Turn the rock over to reveal the word Bethel.

*Place **Object #5** (two wedding veils) on the underlay as you mention each wedding.*

WORDS

When Esau returned with stew for his father, he discovered that Isaac had been tricked into giving away the blessing that should have been his. He was angry and threatened to kill Jacob. Rebekah asked Isaac to send Jacob away to her family to find a wife. Isaac agreed.

Jacob set off quickly through the desert towards Haran, where his mother's family lived. One night, he found a rock and made it his pillow. While he slept, he dreamt of a great ladder stretching all the way into heaven. There were angels climbing up and down the ladder and God seemed to be above and around and beside the place. A voice said:

"I am the God of Abraham and Isaac. I will give this land on which you lie to you and to your descendants. Through them all the world will be blessed. I am with you, and I will bring you back to this land."

When Jacob awoke, he knew he had heard God in his dream! He poured oil on the stone so that he would always remember what God had said and named the place *Bethel*—the house of God.

Jacob traveled on and came to a well where the shepherds watered their flocks. There was a beautiful young woman there with her father's sheep. She was Rachel, the daughter of his mother's brother. Jacob wanted to make her his wife, so he offered to work for her father Laban for seven years in exchange for his permission to marry Rachel.

After seven years the wedding took place. When Jacob saw his wife's face, he discovered that *he* had been tricked, and that he was married to Leah, Rachel's sister. Laban told Jacob that he could marry Rachel too, if he worked another seven years. Finally Jacob and Rachel were married. Then Jacob worked seven more years for his uncle Laban. In all this time, God blessed Jacob and his work, and Laban's flocks grew.

Jacob worked for his uncle for twenty-one years. Then God came close to him and told him it was time to return home. Jacob packed up all that he had and began the journey home with his family.

Jacob was afraid to meet his brother again. Esau had threatened to kill him and was coming to meet him with 400 men! Jacob prayed to God and sent presents to Esau.

MOVEMENTS

*When you speak of Jacob going apart to pray, place **Object #6** (wooden sign reading Peniel) on the underlay. Take Jacob from the beginning of the lesson and place him on the sign. Cover him with your hand when you speak of the man wrestling with him all through the night. After you say, "And he blessed him," remove your hand.*

WORDS

That night he went apart from his family to pray. A strange thing happened. Someone struggled with him all night.

WOODEN SIGN ON UNDERLAY (STORYTELLER'S PERSPECTIVE)

The stranger touched Jacob's thigh and his hip came out of joint. But Jacob held on until morning. The stranger said "Let me go." But Jacob knew this was no ordinary person. He refused to let go until the stranger had given him a blessing. The stranger said: "Your name will no longer be Jacob. You will be called Israel—for you have struggled with God and with people and have prevailed." And he blessed him. So Jacob called the place *Peniel,* which means "the face of God," because he knew he had been struggling with God.

Jacob caught up with his family, limping because of his injury. Then he went in front of them to meet Esau. He bowed down to the ground as Esau came near. Then his brother ran to him and put his arms around him.

Finally old Isaac died, and his sons Esau and Jacob buried him.

*Place **Object #7** (12 People of God—one for each of Jacob's sons) on the underlay as you mention each son.*

Jacob, or Israel as he was now called, had twelve sons. Each of these sons became the head of a tribe. Now there were twelve tribes in the Great Family, and it was called *Israel.*

MOVEMENTS   WORDS

FINAL LAYOUT OF THE STORY OF JACOB (CHILDREN'S PERSPECTIVE)

Sit for a moment and look at the lesson from beginning to end to let the story rest. Then begin the wondering.

I wonder what part of this story you like the best?

I wonder what part is the most important?

I wonder what part is about you or what part you were in?

I wonder if we can leave out any of the story and still have all that we need?

After the wondering is over, show the children the control card for them to use to check their own telling of the story. Then put the story away carefully. Pick up each object in reverse order and remind the children what the object is, saying for example, "Here are the twelve sons of Jacob." After all of the objects are back in the tray, carefully model how to roll the underlay back up and place it in the tray as well. Return the lesson to its place on the shelf. Then return to your spot in the circle and dismiss the children one by one to their work.

LESSON 5

THE STORY OF JOSEPH

LESSON NOTES

FOCUS: JOSEPH: A LEADER, DREAMER AND INTERPRETER OF DREAMS (GENESIS 37:1-31; 49:1-6)

- ● SACRED STORY
- ● ENRICHMENT PRESENTATION

THE MATERIAL

- ● LOCATION: OLD TESTAMENT SACRED STORY SHELVES, BOTTOM SHELF, UNDER "SARAH"
- ● PIECES: SMALL BASKET WITH 12 PEOPLE OF GOD IN IT (ONE FOR EACH OF THE 12 SONS OF JACOB), COAT OF MANY COLORS, 12 HEADS OF GRAIN, IMAGE OF SUN, MOON AND STARS FROM "CREATION," CLEAR BOX FILLED WITH SILVER COINS, PYRAMID, COW AND EAR OF CORN, SACK OF GRAIN
- ● CONTROL
- ● UNDERLAY: TAN FELT STRIP, 42" X 11"

BACKGROUND

The story of Joseph adds to the core narrative of the journey of the people of God from the beginning of "the Great Family" to the Exodus. Why did the People of God move to Egypt and become slaves? It was because of a famine in their land. There was also a famine in the land of Egypt, but they had stored up grain during the good years so there was food there. Why did they store the grain? Because of Joseph's leadership. Here is his story.

NOTES ON THE MATERIAL

Joseph's story sits in a deep wooden or wicker tray (12" x 8" x 3"). The story icon (5" x 2.5") is Joseph's coat of many colors. It can be attached to the end or the side of the tray depending on the size of the shelves, the classroom or other considerations. The underlay is a strip of tan felt, 42" x 11". Each object in the story is approximately the same size (no more than 4" high and 4" wide). The story calls for the following objects: a small basket containing twelve People of God (Jacob's twelve sons), a small coat of many colors, twelve heads of grain, the image of the sun, moon and stars from the Creation story (*Volume 2*, p. 41), clear box filled with silver coins, a small gold pyramid, a cow and ear of corn, and a sack of grain.

A control for the lesson is folded and placed in the tray for the children to use to check their work. The sequence of the story is important because when you change the sequence, you change the story.

SPECIAL NOTES

The core stories about the People of God are placed on the top of the sacred story shelves. The enrichment stories about the key people in the core stories are placed on the lower shelves of the sacred story section in the room, under the core stories they enrich and extend (see diagram below).

The story of Joseph adds to the core narrative the journey of the people of God from the beginning of "the Great Family" to the Exodus. When you introduce the stories in this volume, take care to set them in the larger context of the sacred story of which they are a part. You can accomplish this by:
• presenting the top shelf story the week before and then following up with this,
• presenting the top shelf story briefly on the same day you present this, or
• standing by the shelf and reminding the children of the top shelf story before bringing this one to the circle.

As you tell the story of Jacob's life, place objects on the underlay to remind you of each important event. Unroll the underlay slowly, just enough for the next object, as if you are unrolling a life. At the end of the wondering, show the children the control card and then carefully place each object back in the tray saying something about each event like, "Here is Jacob's coat of many colors," and so forth. Lastly, model how to roll the underlay back up and place it in the tray.

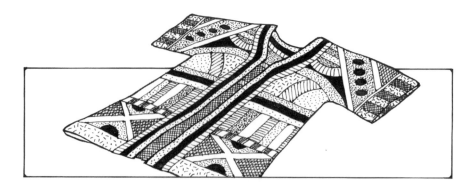

STORY ICON FOR THE STORY OF JOSEPH

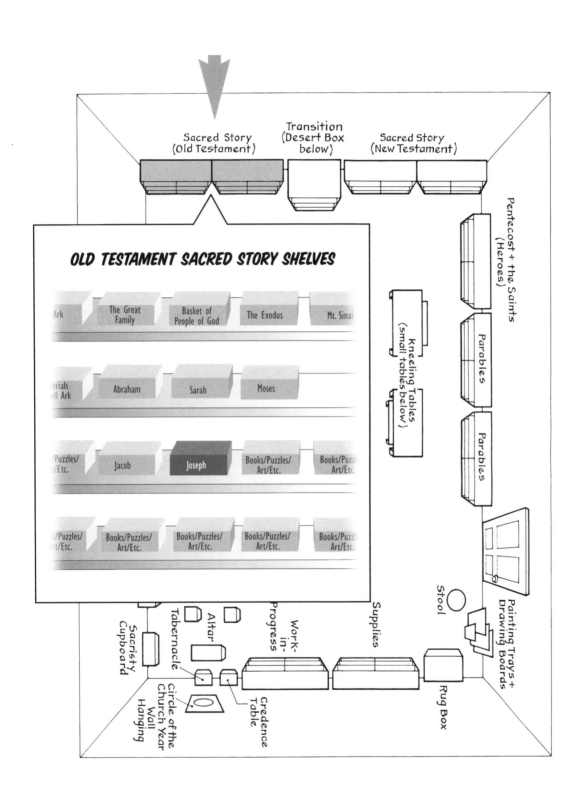

OLD TESTAMENT SACRED STORY SHELVES

Transition (Desert Box below)

Sacred Story (Old Testament)

Sacred Story (New Testament)

Pentecost + the Saints (Heroes)

Parables

Parables

Kneeling Tables (small tables below)

Ark | The Great Family | Basket of People of God | The Exodus | Mt. Sinai

Materials / Shell Ark | Abraham | Sarah | Moses

Books/Puzzles/Art/Etc. | Jacob | Joseph | Books/Puzzles/Art/Etc. | Books/Puzzles/Art/Etc.

Books/Puzzles/Art/Etc. | Books/Puzzles/Art/Etc. | Books/Puzzles/Art/Etc. | Books/Puzzles/Art/Etc. | Books/Puzzles/Art/Etc.

Sacristy Cupboard

Tabernacle

Altar

Work-in-Progress

Supplies

Stool

Painting Trays + Drawing Boards

Rug Box

Circle of the Church Year Wall Hanging

Credence Table

WHERE TO FIND MATERIALS (TEACHING OBJECTS)

MOVEMENTS	WORDS
Move with deliberation to the shelf where the material waits.	⬤ Watch. Watch where I go.
Pick up the tray containing the material and return to the circle. You may need to say:	⬤ Everyone needs to be ready.
Remove the underlay from the tray and unroll it so that just the first object will fit, right to left (storyteller's perspective).	
*Place **Object #1** (twelve People of God—one for each of the sons of Jacob) on the underlay.*	⬤ The Great Family grew. Jacob had twelve sons.
*Place **Object #2** (long-sleeved coat of many colors) on the underlay.*	⬤ Jacob's favorite son was Joseph. To show his love, Jacob gave Joseph a long-sleeved coat with many colors. This made Joseph's brothers hate him.
*Place **Object #3** (twelve heads of grain) on the underlay.*	⬤ One night, Joseph had a dream. He and his brothers were working in a field gathering wheat. Suddenly, Joseph's bundle rose up and all of his brother's bowed down before his. Joseph told his brothers this dream and they hated him even more. They wondered if Joseph would rule over them.
*Place **Object #4** (image of sun, moon and stars) on the underlay.*	⬤ Joseph had another dream. In this dream, the sun, moon and eleven stars bowed down before him. Joseph told his father and brothers about this dream, and they all became angry. It sounded like not only the brothers, but also Jacob and his wife would bow down before Joseph.
	One day, when the brothers were far away in the fields with the flocks, Jacob sent Joseph to see how they were doing. Joseph went to them, and when his brothers saw him coming, they decided to kill him, but the oldest brother, Reuben, convinced them not to. Instead, they took away his coat and put him into a pit.
*Place **Object #5** (clear box filled with twenty pieces of silver/coins) on the underlay*	⬤ Soon, a caravan of traders came past. The brothers sold Joseph to the traders for twenty pieces of silver. They took Joseph's coat and dipped it in the blood of a goat, and brought the coat to their father. They told Jacob that a wild beast had killed Joseph, and Jacob wept.

MOVEMENTS	WORDS
*Place **Object #6** (pyramid) on the underlay.*	Joseph was taken to Egypt and sold as a slave. A captain of the Pharaoh's army named Potiphar purchased him. Potiphar's wife had Joseph sent to jail, but Joseph remained close to God and God to him. Some of the Pharaoh's servants were in jail with Joseph. They had dreams and Joseph told them what they meant.
	When the Pharaoh's servants were released they found that the Pharaoh had dreamed many dreams that no one understood. One of them told Pharaoh about Joseph, and Pharaoh called for him.
*Place **Object #7** (cow and ear of corn) on the underlay when you mention them.*	The Pharaoh's dream had two parts. First there were seven fat cows and seven skinny cows. The thin cows ate the fat ones. Then he dreamed there were seven fat and good ears of corn and seven sick and thin ones. The thin ones swallowed up the good ones.
	Joseph told the Pharaoh that his dreams meant that there would be seven good years followed by seven bad years. He told Pharaoh that this was a warning to save up grain during the good years so that there would be food for the people of Egypt in the bad years. Pharaoh agreed and put Joseph in charge of gathering and saving the grain. Joseph was now thirty years old.
	The lands near Egypt also had bad years. The people from the lands near Egypt came to Joseph to beg for food. Jacob sent ten of his sons into Egypt to get food to eat.
*Place **Object #8** (sack of grain) on the underlay.*	When the brothers came to Egypt, they bowed down before Joseph They did not recognize him, but Joseph knew who they were. He kept one of the brothers with him and gave the others grain, and told them to go home.
	Then all of them came back. This time Joseph told them who he was. He said, "God sent me before you to preserve life."
	Joseph and his family spent the rest of their days in Egypt. When Jacob died Joseph took him home to be buried in the land of their fathers. Then Joseph and his brothers returned to Egypt, where years later their children would become slaves because the new Pharaoh forgot all that Joseph did.

MOVEMENTS   WORDS

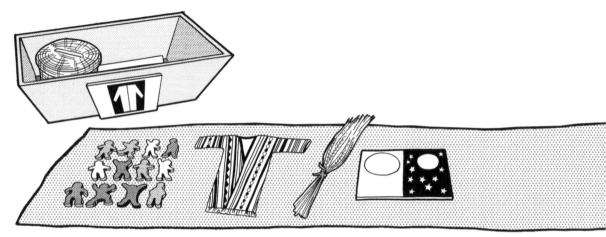

FINAL LAYOUT OF THE STORY OF JOSEPH (CHILDREN'S PERSPECTIVE)

Sit for a moment and look at the lesson from beginning to end to let the story rest. Then begin the wondering.

I wonder what part of the story you like the best?

I wonder what part is the most important?

I wonder what part is about you or what part was especially for you?

I wonder if we can leave out any of the story and still have all that we need?

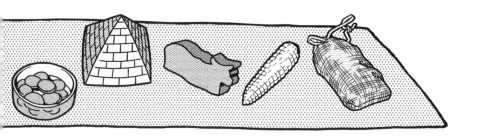

After the wondering is over, show the children the control card for them to use to check their own telling of the story. Then put the story away carefully. Pick up each object in reverse order and remind the children what the object is, saying for example, "Here is Joseph's coat of many colors." After all of the objects are back in the tray, carefully model how to roll the underlay back up and place it in the tray as well. Return the lesson to its place on the shelf. Then return to your spot in the circle and dismiss the children one by one to their work.

THE STORY OF MOSES

LESSON NOTES

FOCUS: THE ONE WHO WAS DRAWN OUT OF THE REEDS BY AN EGYPTIAN PRINCESS TO DRAW THE PEOPLE OF GOD OUT OF EGYPT (EXODUS 1:8-17:7; 19:1-40:38; DEUTERONOMY 34:8)

- SACRED STORY
- ENRICHMENT PRESENTATION

THE MATERIAL

- LOCATION: OLD TESTAMENT SACRED STORY SHELVES, MIDDLE SHELF, UNDER "THE EXODUS"
- PIECES: BABY MOSES IN BASKET AND REEDS TO COVER IT, BURNING BUSH, 2 PIECES OF "FELT WATER" TO SHOW THE PARTING OF THE RED SEA, 2 QUAIL, "MANNA" IN CLEAR BOX, STAFF AND ROCK, MT. SINAI FROM THE TOP SHELF, GOLDEN CALF, BROKEN TEN COMMANDMENT TABLETS, ARK OF THE COVENANT
- CONTROL
- UNDERLAY: TAN FELT STRIP, 42" X 11"

BACKGROUND

The story of Moses enriches the Exodus (*Volume 2*, p. 65), the Ten Best Ways (*Volume 2*, p. 73) and the Ark and the Tent (*Volume 2*, p. 91). The princess who rescued Moses from the river Nile gave him an Egyptian name that is translated by the Hebrew verb "to draw out." He was drawn out from the reeds of the Nile by the daughter of the Pharaoh to draw the people of God out of bondage in Egypt.

When Moses came down from Mt. Sinai, his face was shining after his being so close to God and God being so close to him. The same thing happened when he went into the Tabernacle to pray (Exodus 35:29-35). He was in the wilderness for forty years as a shepherd working for his wife's father, Jethro, a priest of Midian. Then he was in the wilderness another forty years before his death on Mt. Nebo where he looked over the river Jordan to see the Promised Land, but he could not cross over.

NOTES ON THE MATERIAL

Moses' story sits in a deep wooden or wicker tray (12" x 8" x 3"). The story icon (5" x 2.5") is the burning bush. It can be attached to the end or the side of the tray depending on the size of the shelves, the classroom or other considerations. The underlay is a strip of tan felt, 42" x 11". Each object in the story is approximately the same size (no more than 4" high and 4" wide). The story calls for the following objects: a small baby wrapped in a blanket and placed in a small basket, green felt "reeds," a burning bush, two pieces of blue felt (7" x 3") to represent the Red Sea, 2 quail, a rock and a shepherd's staff, Mt. Sinai from the top shelf, a golden calf, 10 commandment tablets split in two and the Ark of the Covenant (like the one used in the story "The Ark and the Tent," *Volume 2, p. 81*). A control for the lesson is folded and placed in the tray for the children to use to check their work. The sequence of the story is important because when you change the sequence, you change the story.

SPECIAL NOTES

The core stories about the People of God are placed on the top of the sacred story shelves. The enrichment stories about the key people in the core stories are placed on the lower shelves of the sacred story section in the room, under the core stories they enrich and extend (see diagram below).

Moses' story enriches the Exodus, the Ten Best Ways, and the Ark and the Tent. When you introduce the stories in this volume, take care to set them in the larger context of the sacred story of which they are a part.

As you tell the story of Moses' life place objects on the underlay to remind you of each important event. Unroll the underlay slowly, just enough for each object, as if you are unrolling a life. At the end of the wondering, show the children the control card and then carefully place each object back in the tray saying something about each event like, "Here is Mount Nebo," and so forth. Lastly, model how to roll the underlay back up and place it in the tray.

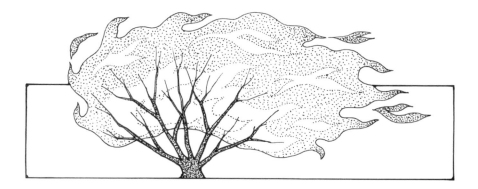

STORY ICON FOR THE STORY OF MOSES

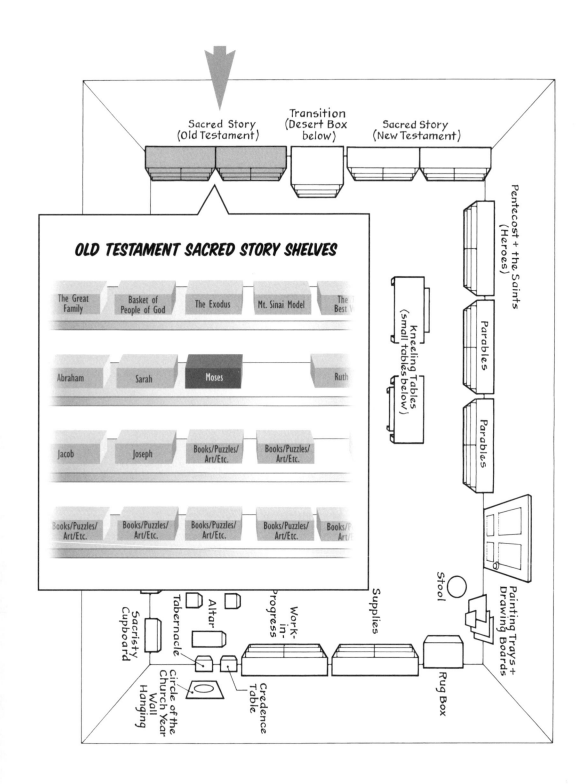

WHERE TO FIND MATERIALS (TEACHING OBJECTS)

MOVEMENTS	WORDS
Move with deliberation to the shelf where the material waits.	Watch. Watch where I go.
Pick up the tray containing the material and return to the circle. Then say:	We need something else.
Go and get the mountain from the shelf.	
You may need to say:	Everyone needs to be ready.
Take the underlay out of the tray. Unroll it so that the first object will fit, right to left (the storyteller's perspective).	After many years a new Pharaoh ruled. He did not remember what Joseph had done for Egypt. The People of God became slaves. They were trapped and could not go home.

There were so many of the People of God in Egypt that the Pharaoh was afraid they would take his kingdom away from him, so he said that all the baby boys had to be killed. |
| *Place **Object #1** (Baby Moses in basket) on the underlay. Slowly cover it with the green felt reeds.* | One of the mothers made a basket of bulrushes woven together and hid the baby in the basket. She put the basket in the reeds by the Nile.

The daughter of the Pharaoh found the basket. She named the baby *Moses* and raised him in the palace.

When Moses was a young man, he saw an Egyptian beating one of the People of God. Moses grew angry and killed him. Then he ran away into the desert.

Moses stayed with the family of Jethro. He married Zepporah, one of Jethro's daughters, and became a shepherd. He lived there for forty years. |
| *Place **Object #2** (burning bush) on the underlay as you speak of it.* | One day while Moses was taking care of Jethro's sheep, he took them to the mountain of God, Mt. Horeb, which is also called Sinai. Suddenly he saw a bush that was burning but did not burn up. |

MOVEMENTS	WORDS
	God spoke to Moses from the burning bush. God told Moses that the cries of the People of God in Egypt had been heard. Moses was to go and set the people free.
	Moses said, "But who am I to do such a thing?"
	God said, "I will be with you."
	"What is your name?"
	"My name is Yahweh. I am who I am."
	"Can't you send someone else?"
	"Aaron, your brother, will go with you. He will speak for you."
	So Moses went back to Egypt to tell the Pharaoh to let his people go. Moses went many times to the Pharaoh to tell him to let God's people go, and many times the Pharaoh said, "No!" Terrible things happened in the land of Egypt. Finally the Pharaoh said, "Yes."
*Place **Object #3** (felt water) on the underlay and unroll it to show the parting of the waters. Move one of your fingers through the opening to show how the people went through.*	God helped Moses lead the people through the water into freedom.

FELT WATER SHOWING THE PARTING OF THE WATERS (STORYTELLER'S PERSPECTIVE)

MOVEMENTS

*Place **Object #4**: (quail and manna) on the underlay as you speak of them.*

__Object #5__ (staff and rock): Place the rock on the underlay and hold the staff over it as you tell this part. Then place the staff on the underlay beside the rock.

*Place **Object #6** (Mt. Sinai from the top shelf) on the underlay.*

*Place **Object #7** (golden calf) on the underlay.*

*Place **Object #8** (broken tablets) on the underlay.*

WORDS

Moses led the people through the desert for 40 years. The People of God grew tired and hungry and discouraged—and they grumbled to Moses.

But God showed the people that God was with them by giving them quail and manna to eat in the desert.

When the people were thirsty from traveling in the desert, they complained to Moses, and Moses talked with God. God told Moses to strike a rock with his staff. Water came out of the rock so the people could drink.

Something happened that made God angry. Moses did not keep faith with God in the midst of the people, so God told Moses that he would see but never enter the Promised Land (Exodus 17:1-7, Deuteronomy 32:51-52).

The people were free. But they didn't know the best way to go. With God's help, Moses led the people to God's mountain, Mt. Sinai, where God had spoken to him from the burning bush. And Moses went up on the mountain to talk with God. The people waited...and waited...and waited. Moses was gone a long time.

The people began to think Moses was never coming back, so they asked Aaron to make them a new god to lead them. Aaron took all of the gold the women were wearing and melted it. Then he shaped the melted gold into a calf. He gave the calf to the people saying, "Here is your god." And the people built an altar and worshiped the golden calf.

Moses came down from the mountain; his face was shining. He carried the Ten Best Ways, but found the people worshiping the golden calf. He grew angry and broke the stone tablets on which the Ten Best Ways were written. He took the golden calf and threw it in the fire. The people were sorry, so God gave Moses the Ten Best Ways again, and Moses gave them to the people.

MOVEMENTS

*Place **Object #9** (Ark of the Covenant) on the underlay. Cover the Ark with your hands when you speak of the tent.*

Touch the underlay with respect when you speak of Moses' being buried.

WORDS

God told Moses to have the people make a box called an ark to hold the Ten Best Ways. The box was covered with gold, and it had poles on the sides, so the people could always carry it with them wherever they went. God told Moses how to make a tent called a tabernacle for the ark. When the people stopped to rest in the wilderness God's glory filled the tent, and Moses came close to God there. When he came out his face was shining.

After forty years, they came to another Mountain, Mt. Nebo. Moses looked over into the Promised land from the mountain-top, and God said, "I will give this land to the People of God, but you will not cross over."

Moses died there and no one knows to this day where he was buried.

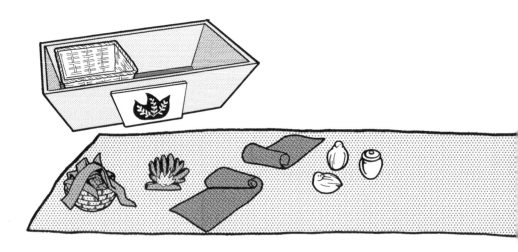

FINAL LAYOUT OF THE STORY OF MOSES

MOVEMENTS

Sit for a moment and look at the lesson from beginning to end to let the story rest. Then begin the wondering.

After the wondering is over, show the children the control card for them to to use to check their own telling of the story. Then put the story away carefully. Pick up each object in reverse order and remind the children what the object is, saying for example, "Here is the burning bush." After all of the objects are back in the tray, carefully model how to roll the underlay back up and place it in the tray as well. Return the lesson to its place on the shelf. Then return to your spot in the circle and dismiss the children one by one to their work.

WORDS

I wonder what part of the story you like the best?

I wonder what part is the most important?

I wonder what part is about you or what part was especially for you?

I wonder if we can leave out any of the story and still have all that we need?

THE STORY OF RUTH

LESSON NOTES

FOCUS: THE MOABITE GREAT-GRANDMOTHER OF DAVID, WHO WORKED HARD, LOVED GOD, AND GOD'S PEOPLE (THE BOOK OF RUTH)

- SACRED STORY
- ENRICHMENT PRESENTATION

THE MATERIAL

- LOCATION: OLD TESTAMENT SACRED STORY SHELVES, MIDDLE SHELF, UNDER "THE TEN BEST WAYS"
- PIECES: MODEL OF BETHLEHEM, PEOPLE OF GOD (9 TOTAL), STALKS OF GRAIN, CROWN, BLUE YARN
- UNDERLAY: DARK BROWN FELT, 22" X 36"

BACKGROUND

The story of Ruth is a connecting story. It connects the wilderness experience of the People of God and living in the promised land, with living in the promised land and King David. Ruth was not one of the People of God. She was a Moabite. She married one of God's people, Boaz, and became the great-grandmother of David the King.

The Hebrew Bible is organized into Torah, Prophets, and Writings. The Book of Ruth is included among the Writings. It presents a peaceful contrast to the political chaos, scarcity and cruelty of the time of the judges.

NOTES ON THE MATERIAL

Ruth's story sits in a deep wooden or wicker tray (12" x 8" x 3"). The story icon (5" x 2.5") is an image of Ruth gathering wheat. It can be attached to the end or the side of the tray depending on the size of the shelves, the classroom or other considerations. The underlay is a large piece of dark brown felt, 22" x 36". The story calls for the following objects: a long piece of yarn (about 42" long so you can place it on the underlay in a squiggly line to represent the Jordan River, a small model of Bethlehem (like the one used in "Advent I-IV," *Volume 3*, approximately 4" tall), nine People of God, stalks of grain and a crown.

SPECIAL NOTES

The core stories about the People of God are placed on the top of the sacred story shelves. The enrichment stories about the key people in the core stories are placed on the lower shelves of the sacred story section in the room, under the core stories they enrich and extend (see diagram below).

When you introduce the stories in this volume, take care to set them in the larger context of the sacred story of which they are a part. You can accomplish this by:
• presenting the top shelf story the week before and then following up with this,
• presenting the top shelf story briefly on the same day you present this, or
• standing by the shelf and reminding the children of the top shelf story before bringing this one to the circle.

Ruth's story does not unroll like a life in the way that the other stories in this volume do. The movement of the story is instead from the Promised Land, specifically the city of Bethlehem, to the land of Moab, and back again.

STORY ICON FOR THE STORY OF RUTH

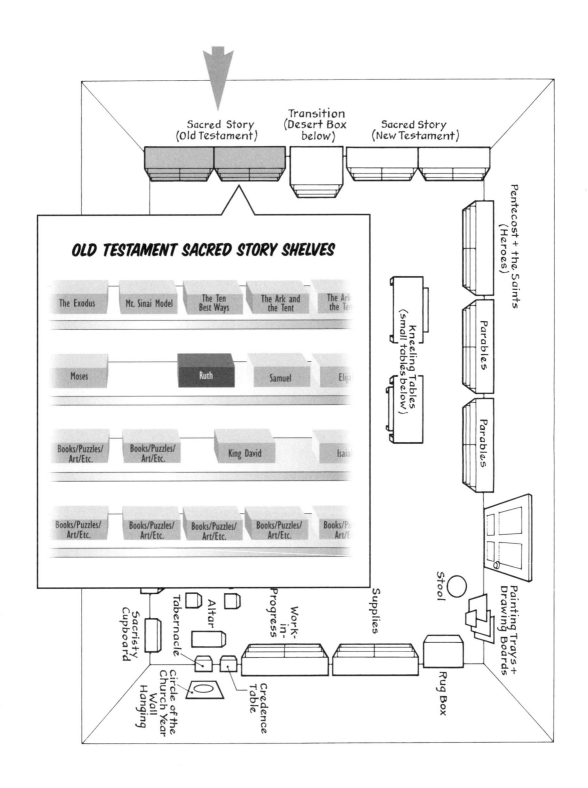

WHERE TO FIND MATERIALS (TEACHING OBJECTS)

MOVEMENTS	WORDS
Move with deliberation to the shelf where the material waits.	Watch. Watch where I go.
Pick up the tray containing the material and return to the circle.	
You may need to say:	Everyone needs to be ready.
Take the underlay out of the tray and spread it out. Place the blue yarn down the middle in a squiggly line to represent the Jordan River, which actually does twist and turn like this.	
Move your hand from your left to the right of the river, placing it on the dark brown underlay as you say, "They filled the land." Place four of the People of God in the Land. Then place the model of Bethlehem between the people and you.	After the People of God crossed over the Jordan River, into the Promised Land, they filled the land. Some of them began to live in Bethlehem.

**THE MODEL OF BETHLEHEM
(STORYTELLER'S PERSPECTIVE)**

Show with your hand the land of Moab—to the right of the river from the storyteller's perspective. Move the four People of God (Naomi, her husband and their two sons) across the river into Moab.	Many years went by. Then a time came when there was no rain so the wheat could not grow. Some of the people decided to cross over the Jordan River to Moab where there was food. Naomi, her husband and their two sons, were among those who went.
Take away one person.	In this new land they were happy, until Naomi's husband died. That was very sad.

MOVEMENTS	**WORDS**
Add two people as you name Orpah and Ruth.	⏵ Later her two sons married young women from Moab. Their names were Orpah and Ruth.
Take away two sons.	⏵ When these husbands died, Naomi, Ruth and Orpah were all widows together.

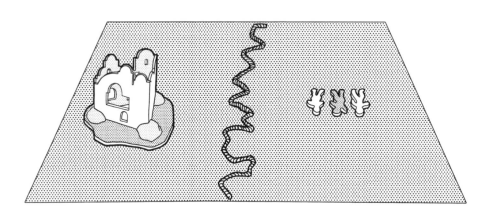

THE LAYOUT WITHOUT THE TWO SONS (STORYTELLER'S PERSPECTIVE)

Move Orpah away from the other two.	⏵ Naomi didn't know what to do, so she decided to go back across the desert to her family in Bethlehem. Orpah went to live with her mother in Moab.
Put your hand on Ruth as you say, "Where you go…"	⏵ Ruth stayed with Naomi. She said, "Where you go, I will go. Where you live, I will live. Your people shall be my people, and your God, my God."
Move Naomi and Ruth back across the river to Bethlehem.	⏵ Then they traveled to Bethlehem where they found a small place to live.
Place the stalks of grain beside Naomi and Ruth.	⏵ They went into the nearby fields to gather grain left after the harvest. People let them do that because they were widows.
Place another person on the underlay beside Ruth to represent Boaz. Move Boaz close to Ruth and Naomi a little away.	⏵ One of the fields belonged to Boaz, a rich man. He saw Ruth. He liked how she worked hard and took care of Naomi.
Place another person on the underlay to represent Ruth and Boaz's son.	⏵ In time they were married and had children. Now Ruth was a mother and Naomi was a grandmother. She could hold her grandson on her lap.

MOVEMENTS

Place another person on the underlay to represent Jesse and then one for David. Put the crown beside David.

WORDS

When the little boy grew up he had a son, Jesse, and Jesse had many sons. One of Jesse's sons grew up to be the great King David. He was the great grandson of Ruth.

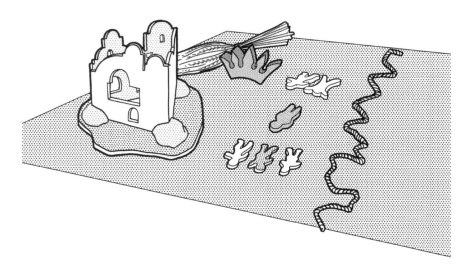

THE LAYOUT WITH JESSE AND THE CROWN IN PLACE (STORYTELLER'S PERSPECTIVE)

Sit for a moment and look at the lesson from beginning to end to let the story rest. Then begin the wondering.

I wonder what part of this story you liked the best?

I wonder what part was the most important?

I wonder what part was about you or what part you were in?

I wonder what part we could leave out and still have all the story that we need?

Carefully return everything to the tray. Model how to fold the underlay so it fits nicely in the tray. Return the story to its place on the shelves. Return to your place in the circle and begin to dismiss the children to their work.

THE STORY OF SAMUEL

LESSON NOTES

FOCUS: THE STORY OF SAMUEL; PROPHET, PRIEST AND JUDGE (1 SAMUEL 1-28:3).

- SACRED STORY
- ENRICHMENT PRESENTATION

THE MATERIAL

- LOCATION: OLD TESTAMENT SACRED STORY SHELVES, MIDDLE SHELF, UNDER "THE ARK AND THE TENT"
- PIECES: ARK OF THE COVENANT, WRAPPED PRESENT, 3 COATS, SLEEPING MAT, SMALL CLEAR BOTTLE OF OIL, CROWN
- CONTROL
- UNDERLAY: DARK BROWN FELT STRIP, 42" X 11"

BACKGROUND

The story of Samuel connects worship in God's tent (the tabernacle complex) and worship in God's temple. I and II Samuel were one book in Hebrew. Samuel's story is in I Samuel, with Saul's story, and David's story begins midway through I Samuel and continues through II Samuel. Samuel was an early prophet and the last of the judges to rule the twelve tribes of Israel. He anointed Saul and then David as kings to rule after him.

NOTES ON THE MATERIAL

Samuel's story sits in a deep wooden or wicker tray (12" x 8" x 3"). The story icon (5"x 2.5") is "a horn of oil," like what Samuel would have used to anoint first King Saul and then David. It can be attached to the end or the side of the tray depending on the size of the shelves, the classroom or other considerations. The underlay is a strip of dark brown felt, 42" x 11". Each object in the story is approximately the same size (no more than 4" high and 4" wide). The story calls for the following objects: the Ark of the Covenant (like the one used in the lesson on the top shelf, "The Ark and the Tent," *Volume 2*, p. 81), a baby wrapped in a blanket, three coats each a little larger than the next showing Samuel's growth as a child, a mat for sleeping, a bottle of oil for anointing, a crown.

A control for the lesson is folded and placed in the tray for the children to use to check their work. The sequence of the story is important because when you change the sequence, you change the story.

SPECIAL NOTES

The core stories about the People of God are placed on the top of the sacred story shelves. The enrichment stories about the key people in the core stories are placed on the lower shelves of the sacred story section in the room, under the core stories they enrich and extend (see diagram below).

When you introduce the stories in this volume, take care to set them in the larger context of the sacred story of which they are a part. You can accomplish this by:
• presenting the top shelf story the week before and then following up with this,
• presenting the top shelf story briefly on the same day you present this, or
• standing by the shelf and reminding the children of the top shelf story before bringing this one to the circle.

As you tell the story of Samuel, you place objects on the underlay to remind you of each important event. Unroll the underlay slowly, providing just enough space for each object as it's presented, as if you are unrolling a life. At the end of the wondering, show the children the control card and then carefully place each object back in the tray saying something about each event like, "Here are the coats Hannah brought to Samuel each year," and so forth. Lastly, model how to roll the underlay back up and place it in the tray.

STORY ICON FOR THE STORY OF SAMUEL

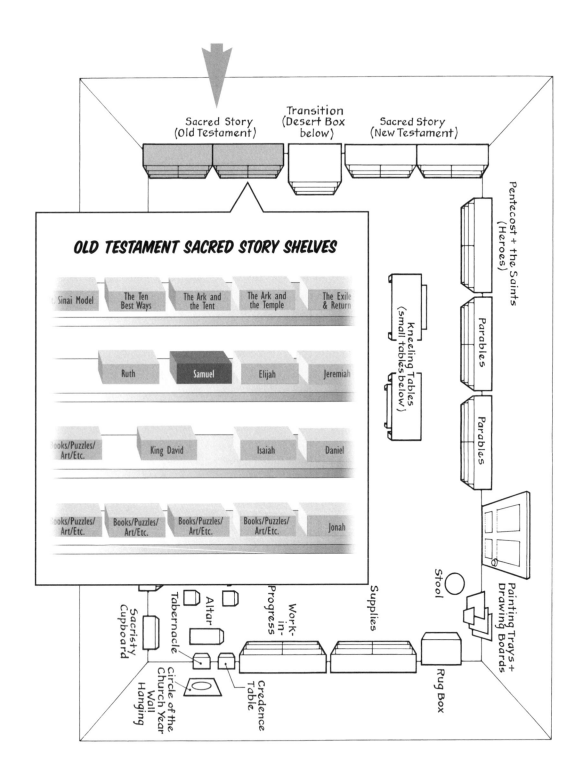

WHERE TO FIND MATERIALS (TEACHING OBJECTS)

MOVEMENTS	WORDS
Move with deliberation to the shelf where the material waits.	Watch. Watch where I go.
Pick up the tray containing the material and return to the circle. You may need to say:	Everyone needs to be ready.
Remove the underlay from the tray and unroll it just enough so that the first object will fit, from right to left (story-teller's perspective).	
*Place **Object #1** (Ark of the Covenant) on the underlay.*	When the People of God came into the Promised Land, they carried the ark into the mountains to a place called Shiloh. They put up the tent for God, and the ark stayed there.
	The People of God settled in the hills around the ark. Two of the people, Hannah and Elkahnah, lived in Ramah not far from where the ark was kept. Each year they came to Shiloh to pray.
	Hannah wanted to be a mother so much, but she had no children. One year she prayed so deeply in front of God's tent that one of the priests named Eli worried. He went to her to see if he could help. She told him that she was asking God to help her have a baby. He helped her pray
*Place **Object #2** Place (baby wrapped in blanket) on the underlay.*	Hannah and Elkanah had a baby, and they named him *Samuel*, which means "someone given by God."
*Place **Object #3** (three coats, each one slightly bigger than the previous one, to mark the passage of time) on the underlay.*	When Samuel was old enough, Hannah and Elkanah brought Samuel to Shiloh to live with Eli and learn how to care for the ark. But every year Hannah came to see him and brought him a new coat to wear.

MOVEMENTS	WORDS
Place **Object #4** (sleeping mat) on the underlay. Move your hand away from the mat three times to show how Samuel got up and went to Eli.	One night when Samuel was asleep on his mat in the tent, God called, "Samuel, Samuel!" Samuel thought it must be Eli calling, so he went to him. But Eli did not call him, and he told Samuel to go lie down. This happened three times, until Eli realized that God must be calling Samuel. He told Samuel to go back and lie down. He said, "If you hear the voice again, say, "Speak, God, for your servant hears."
Leave your hand resting on the mat when you say that Samuel did as Eli told him.	God called him again, but this time Samuel did as Eli told him. God told Samuel that Eli's own sons and the People of God would lose the ark in a battle, and Eli would fall down and die when he heard the news.
	In the morning Samuel told Eli what God had told him. It came true. The People of God lost the ark, and Eli died.
	Since the ark and the priests were gone, Samuel went back to live with his mother and father. But God stayed close to Samuel, and he became the leader of all the people called a judge. He was also a true prophet.
Place **Object #5** (small bottle of oil and crown) on the underlay when you mention the anointing and then the crown.	When Samuel grew old the people came to him and asked for a king. They wanted to be like the other nations. Samuel wasn't sure what to do, so he prayed to God, and God told him to go find a king.
	Samuel began to look for the right person to be king. He knew at once that Saul was the right one. He anointed him king by pouring oil over his head and giving thanks to God.
	Saul led the armies of Israel, and he was their king, but the Spirit of the Lord left Saul.

FINAL LAYOUT OF THE STORY OF SAMUEL (CHILDREN'S PERSPECTIVE)

MOVEMENTS

Object #6: Move the oil for anointing down to the end of the underlay to indicate the second anointing, but leave the crown. (David is not crowned king until after Saul dies.)

Sit for a moment and look at the lesson from beginning to end to let the story rest. Then begin the wondering.

After the wondering is over, show the children the control card for them to use to check their own telling of the story. Then put the story away carefully. Pick up each object in reverse order and remind the children what the object is, saying for example, "Here is the oil Samuel used to anoint Saul the king and then David." After all of the objects are back in the tray, carefully model how to roll the underlay back up and place it in the tray as well. Return the lesson to its place on the shelf. Then return to your spot in the circle and dismiss the children one by one to their work.

WORDS

One day God told Samuel to anoint a new king. He went to the house of the family of Jesse in Bethlehem. There he found David, Jesse's youngest son, and anointed him to be the new king when Saul died.

When all of Samuel's work was finished, he went back home to Ramah. When he died, people from all over Israel gathered to remember him with tears of sadness and thanksgiving.

I wonder what part of this story you liked the best?

I wonder what part is the most important?

I wonder what part is about you?

I wonder if we could leave any of the story out and still have all that we need?

THE STORY OF KING DAVID

LESSON NOTES

FOCUS: DAVID, THE IMPERFECT BUT BELOVED AND REPENTANT KING (1 SAMUEL 16–31, 2 SAMUEL, 1 KINGS 1–2)

- SACRED STORY
- ENRICHMENT PRESENTATION

THE MATERIAL

- LOCATION: OLD TESTAMENT SACRED STORY SHELVES, BOTTOM SHELF, UNDER BOTH "RUTH" AND "SAMUEL"
- PIECES: CLEAR BOTTLE OF OIL, HARP, BASKET (CONTAINING 5 SMOOTH STONES, SLING SHOT AND SHEPHERDS STAFF), 2 PEOPLE OF GOD, CROWN, ARK OF THE COVENANT, PARABLE BOX (CONTAINING 3" X 3" GREEN UNDERLAY, TWO TAN FELT HOUSES, ONE SMALLER THAN THE OTHER, AND 5 SMALL SHEEP), IMAGE OF JERUSALEM
- CONTROL
- UNDERLAY: PURPLE FELT STRIP, 42" X 11"

BACKGROUND

David brings the tent of God into Jerusalem and sets up the possibility of a house for God. David was anointed king by Samuel when he was just a boy, but he would not become the king until King Saul was killed. As a boy he was known for his music and his courage, and later he became a great soldier in Saul's army. As king he continued to fight important battles and made some great mistakes, but was repentant. He established the kingdom of Israel that lasted for 400 years and made the city of Jerusalem another city of David, like Bethlehem.

NOTES ON THE MATERIAL

David's story sits in a deep wooden or wicker tray (12" x 8" x 3"). The story icon (5" x 2.5") is "a crown." It can be attached to the end or the side of the tray depending on the size of the shelves, the classroom or other considerations. The underlay is a strip of purple felt, 42" x 11". Each object in the story is approximately the same size (no more than 4" high and 4" wide). The story calls for the following objects: a clear bottle of oil, a basket (containing five smooth stones, a sling shot and a shepherd's staff), two People of God, a crown (just like the one used in "The Story of Samuel, " p. 74), the Ark of the Covenant, a small gold box similar to the other parable boxes (containing 3" x 3" green underlay, two tan felt houses, one smaller than the other and five small sheep), and an image of Jerusalem.

A control for the lesson is folded and placed in the tray for the children to use to check their work. The sequence of the story is important because when you change the sequence, you change the story.

SPECIAL NOTES

The core stories about the People of God are placed on the top of the sacred story shelves. The enrichment stories about the key people in the core stories are placed on the lower shelves of the sacred story section in the room, under the core stories they enrich and extend (see diagram below).

When you introduce the stories in this volume, take care to set them in the larger context of the sacred story of which they are a part. You can accomplish this by:
• presenting the top shelf story the week before and then following up with this,
• presenting the top shelf story briefly on the same day you present this, or
• standing by the shelf and reminding the children of the top shelf story before bringing this one to the circle.

As you tell the story of David's life place objects on the underlay to remind you of each important event. Unroll the underlay slowly, just enough for each object, as if you are unrolling a life. At the end of the wondering, show the children the control card and then carefully place each object back in the tray saying something about each event like, "Here is the crown they put on David's head after King Saul died," and so forth. Lastly, model how to roll the underlay back up and place it in the tray.

STORY ICON FOR THE STORY OF KING DAVID

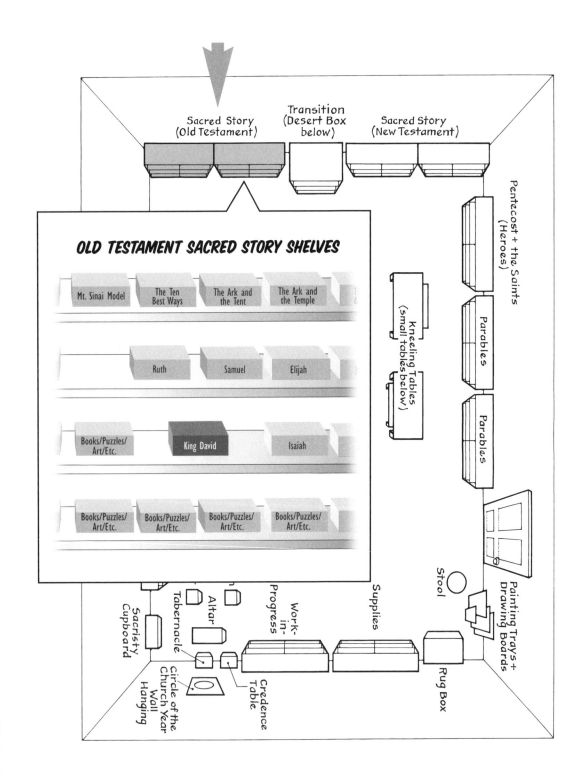

OLD TESTAMENT SACRED STORY SHELVES

| Mt. Sinai Model | The Ten Best Ways | The Ark and the Tent | The Ark and the Temple |

| Ruth | Samuel | Elijah |

| Books/Puzzles/Art/Etc. | King David | Isaiah |

| Books/Puzzles/Art/Etc. | Books/Puzzles/Art/Etc. | Books/Puzzles/Art/Etc. | Books/Puzzles/Art/Etc. |

Sacred Story (Old Testament)

Transition (Desert Box below)

Sacred Story (New Testament)

Pentecost + the Saints (Heroes)

Parables

Parables

kneeling Tables (small tables below)

Stool

Painting Trays + Drawing Boards

Rug Box

Supplies

Work-in-Progress

Credence Table

Circle of the Church Year Wall Hanging

Altar

Tabernacle

Sacristy Cupboard

WHERE TO FIND MATERIALS (TEACHING OBJECTS)

MOVEMENTS	WORDS
Move with deliberation to the shelf where the material waits.	Watch. Watch where I go.
Pick up the tray containing the material and return to the circle.	
As you return to your place in the circle you may need to say:	Everyone needs to be ready.
Take the underlay out of the tray and unroll it just enough so that the first object will fit, from right to left (story-teller's perspective).	
*Place **Object #1** (container of oil) on the underlay.*	In the city of Bethlehem where Ruth had lived, Jesse made his home. Jesse was the grandson of Ruth, and he had many sons. One day Samuel came to Bethlehem in search of a new king. Samuel came to the house of Jesse because God told him that the King would be there. Jesse brought six of his sons to Samuel, but the new king was not among them. Samuel asked, "Are there any more sons?" Jesse said, "Yes, there is David, the youngest, who is keeping the sheep." When Samuel saw him he knew at once that David was the king he was looking for.
Pick up the container of oil and pretend to pour some out onto your hand to anoint David.	He took his horn full of oil like the oil in this container and poured it over David's head to make him the new king. This was very confusing, because there was already a king in the land, King Saul. But Saul had changed. An evil spirit tormented him. Still, David would not begin to rule until Saul died.
*Place **Object #2** (harp) on the underlay.*	Saul's sickness became worse. Someone suggested he needed music to feel better. So David the shepherd boy was brought to play the harp and sing songs to soothe the king. Some of David's songs can be found in the book of the Psalms.
***Object #3:** Take the stones, sling shot and shepherd's staff out of the small basket as each is mentioned in the story and place them on the underlay.*	While David was still a young boy, there was a great war in the land. The Philistines wanted the land for themselves. The army of the People of God and the army of the Philistines were lined up ready to fight.

MOVEMENTS	WORDS
	A very tall man, like a giant, came out to challenge Saul's army. His name was Goliath. No one wanted to fight him. When David heard the challenge, he went forward to fight Goliath. They tried to put the armor of the king on him, but it was too heavy. David cast it aside, and went against Goliath with five smooth stones, his slingshot and his shepherd's staff. He had killed bears and lions to defend the sheep, why couldn't he kill Goliath to defend the people? And he did.
	The people never forgot David's bravery, and when he grew up he became a soldier in the army of the king.
Place **Object #4** (two People of God) on the underlay.	King Saul had many sons. One of them was named Jonathan. David and Jonathan became close friends. Jonathan always stood up for David and tried to protect him from harm even from his father the king. The king was very jealous of David. David was a great soldier and over time he grew more popular than the king himself. This made the king so angry that he wanted to kill David. Jonathan spoke to his father about David and told him that David was a good man, but Saul would not listen. Jonathan knew that the only way for David to be safe would be for him to run away and hide from King Saul. This meant that the two good friends had to say goodbye.
Place **Object #5** (crown) on the underlay as you mention the crown.	King Saul and his sons led their army against the Philistines once more, but this time he and his sons were killed.
	David was moving through the land with his army, and a young man came to him with the news that King Saul and his sons were dead. When David heard the news he was very sad. David never forgot his good friend Jonathan, and later when he was king he brought Jonathan's own son to live with him, to eat at his table, and gave him the land that had belonged to King Saul.
	It was time for David to be king. The young man brought to David the king's crown. All the tribes of Israel came to Hebron and made him king saying, "You shall be shepherd over the people." At the time he was thirty years old and he would be king for forty more years.

MOVEMENTS	WORDS
	One of the first things David did was to go to the City of Jerusalem and take it from the Jebusite people. So now there was a city of David in Bethlehem, and a second one in Jerusalem
Place **Object #6** (Ark of the Covenant) on the underlay.	Then David remembered that the ark had been lost to the Philistines. He led his army against the Philistines and defeated them. They went to get the ark and brought it into Jerusalem. The king danced in front of the ark as it was carried to its place in the tent like it had been in the desert.
	David wanted to build a house for God, a more beautiful place for the ark. But God said, "No." David was king of war. His son Solomon would build the temple.
Object #7: Open the parable box and spread out the underlay.	In the spring of the year, the time when kings go forth to war, David sent his army away, but he remained in Jerusalem. One afternoon he saw Bathsheba, the beautiful wife of Uriah the Hittite. He wanted her for himself, and so he sent Uriah the Hittite into battle where he was killed. Then King David married Bathsheba.
	One day the Lord sent Nathan the prophet to David. Nathan told King David a parable…
Place two houses—the large one for the rich man and the small one for the poor man—on the underlay. Put four of the sheep in front of the rich man's house.	"A rich man and a poor man lived in the same town. The rich man had many sheep.
Put one sheep in front of the poor man's house.	"The poor man had only one little lamb that he raised as a pet in his house. He even let it eat from his plate and drink from his cup. It slept on his lap. The lamb was like one of his own children.
	"One day someone came to visit the rich man. The rich man didn't want to kill any of his own sheep to serve to the visitor, so he took the poor man's lamb and served it instead."

MOVEMENTS

Take away the sheep from in front of the poor man's house and hide it in your hand.

WORDS

David was furious at the rich man in the story. "As the Lord lives, the man who did this deserves to die! He must pay for the lamb four times over because he did this thing and has no pity."

Then Nathan said to David, "*You* are that rich man! God has given you everything and yet you took Uriah's wife for yourself."

David was filled with sorrow. He wondered if he would die, like King Saul. David did not die, but the first son he had with Bathsheba did die. David and Bathsheba were both filled with sorrow, but the next child they had lived. They named him Solomon. He would become the next king and would build a house for God.

King David was not a perfect king...he made many mistakes. But he understood that...and asked God to forgive him. And God did.

*Place **Object #8** (image of Jerusalem) on the underlay.*

When David was old and full of years, he died and was buried in Jerusalem. His son Solomon continued to rule over his kingdom and built the temple.

FINAL LAYOUT OF THE STORY OF DAVID (STORYTELLER'S PERSPECTIVE)

MOVEMENTS

Sit for a moment and look at the lesson from beginning to end to let the story rest. Then begin the wondering.

After the wondering is over, show the children the control card for them to use to check their own telling of the story. Then put the story away carefully. Pick up each object in reverse order and remind the children what the object is, saying for example, "Here Is the parable that Nathan the prophet told King David." After all of the objects are back in the tray, carefully model how to roll the underlay back up and place it in the tray as well. Return the lesson to its place on the shelf. Then return to your spot in the circle and dismiss the children one by one to their work.

WORDS

I wonder what part of this story you liked the best?

I wonder what part was the most important?

I wonder what part was about you, or what part you were in?

I wonder if we could leave any of the story out and still have all the story that we need?

ENRICHMENT LESSON 10

THE STORY OF THE PROPHET ELIJAH

LESSON NOTES

FOCUS: ELIJAH, A CONFRONTER OF KINGS AND ONE WHO COULD HEAR GOD IN THE STILLNESS (1 KINGS 16–19; 2 KINGS 2)

- ● SACRED STORY
- ● ENRICHMENT PRESENTATION

THE MATERIAL

- ● LOCATION: OLD TESTAMENT SACRED STORY SHELVES, MIDDLE SHELF, UNDER "THE ARK AND THE TEMPLE"
- ● PIECES: CROWN, BLACK RAVEN, GRAIN IN SMALL SACK AND CONTAINER OF OIL, 2 WOODEN ALTARS AND 12 STONES, MOUNTAIN FROM THE TOP SHELF, PAINTING OF ELIJAH GOING UP IN HIS CHARIOT OF FIRE
- ● CONTROL
- ● UNDERLAY: DARK BROWN FELT STRIP, 42 " X 11 "

BACKGROUND

This lesson enriches the core story on the Prophets (*Volume 2*, p. 100). Elijah challenged the kings of Israel for their idolatry and immorality. When he died, a whirlwind carried him up into heaven in a fiery chariot. A whirlwind carried him up into heaven. Elisha picked up Elijah's robe and continued Elijah's work. We have no writings from either of these two prophets, but we have their stories in I and II Kings.

NOTES ON THE MATERIALS

Elijah's story sits on a deep wooden or wicker tray (12" x 8" x 3"). The story icon (5" x 2.5") is an image of Elijah in his chariot. It can be attached to the end or the side of the tray depending on the size of the shelves, the classroom or other considerations. The underlay is a strip of dark brown felt, 42" x 11". Each object in the story is approximately the same size (no more than 4" high and 4" wide) except for the mountain which you take from the top shelf. The story calls for the following objects:

a crown, a black raven, grain in small sack and container of oil, two wooden altars and twelve small stones, the mountain from the top shelf and a painting of Elijah going up in his chariot of fire.

A control for the lesson is folded and placed in the tray for the children to use to check their work. The sequence of the story is important because when you change the sequence, you change the story.

SPECIAL NOTES

The core stories about the People of God are placed on the top of the sacred story shelves. The enrichment stories about the key people in the core stories are placed on the lower shelves of the sacred story section in the room, under the core stories they enrich and extend (see diagram below).

Elijah's story enriches the lesson on the Prophets (*Volume 2*, p. 100). When you introduce the stories in this volume, take care to set them in the larger context of the sacred story of which they are a part. You can accomplish this by:
- presenting the top shelf story the week before and then following up with this,
- presenting the top shelf story briefly on the same day you present this, or
- standing by the shelf and reminding the children of the top shelf story before bringing this one to the circle.

As you tell the story of Elijah place objects on the underlay to remind you of each important event. Unroll the underlay slowly, just enough for each object, as if you are unrolling a life. At the end of the wondering, show the children the control card and then carefully place each object back in the tray saying something about each event like, "Here is one of the ravens that fed Elijah by the river," and so forth. Lastly, model how to roll the underlay back up and place it in the tray.

STORY ICON FOR THE STORY OF THE PROPHET ELIJAH

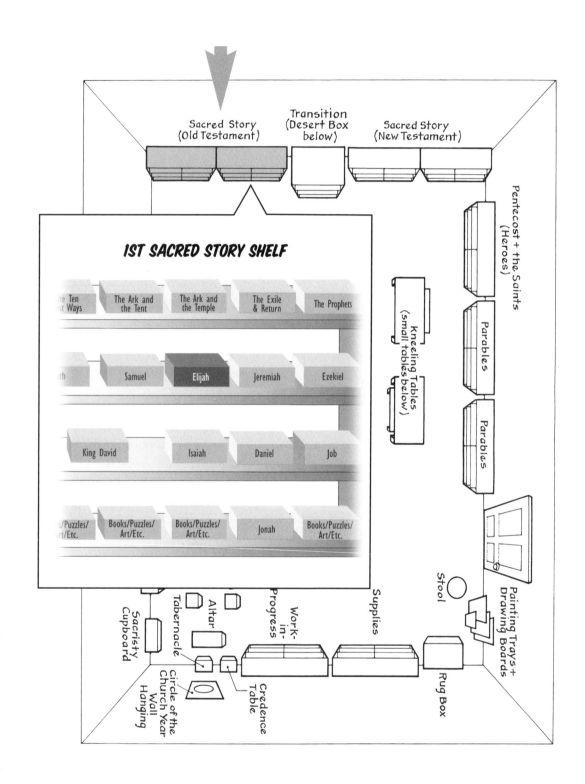

WHERE TO FIND MATERIALS (TEACHING OBJECTS)

MOVEMENTS	**WORDS**
Move with deliberation to the shelf where the material waits.	Watch. Watch where I go.
Pick up the tray containing the material and return to the circle.	
Then go and get the mountain from the top shelf as you say...	Oh...we need one more thing.
As you return to the circle you may need to say...	We need to be ready.
Remove the underlay from the tray and unroll it so that the first object will fit, right to left (the storyteller's perspective).	This is the story of Elijah, the prophet. Prophets are people who come so close to God and God comes so close to them that they know what God wants. When the people do not like the message, they often become very angry with the prophet. It's not easy being a prophet.
*Place **Object #1** (crown) on the underlay.*	There was once a king called Ahab who ruled over Israel. He married a woman called Jezebel from a different land. She persuaded Ahab to worship her god, a god called Baal.
	Ahab even built a temple and placed a statue of Baal in it. He told the Israelites to bow down and worship Baal. God sent the prophet Elijah to warn the king there would be little rain for the next three years because the people were not following God's laws and were worshiping Baal. This made the king very angry, and Elijah had to go into hiding.
*Place **Object #2** (black raven) on the underlay.*	Elijah went to live in the valley of Kerith where there was a running brook. Morning and night, God sent ravens to feed him with bread and meat. And so with both food and water, Elijah was able to stay alive. Still there was no rain in the land, so the brook dried up and Elijah journeyed to a town called Zarephath.
*Place **Object #3** (grain in small sack and container of oil) on the underlay. Touch the sack of flour and oil as you mention them.*	In Zarephath Elijah met a woman gathering sticks for a fire. He asked her for water and bread. The woman told him that all she had was a little flour and oil to make bread, just enough to feed herself and her son. This would be their last meal. Elijah told her to trust in God and if she fed him just a small piece of her bread, the family would never go hungry again. The woman did as Elijah asked, and his promise came true. She was able to feed Elijah and her son for many, many days.

MOVEMENTS

*Place **Object #4** (2 altars) on the underlay, leaving room for the 12 stones (Object #5) to surround the second altar. Place them on the underlay when you mention them.*

*Place **Object #5:** (12 stones) around the second altar.*

WORDS

Three years passed. Elijah returned to speak to the king. Ahab was still angry with Elijah, but he listened because there had been no rain.

Elijah told the king to gather all the priests of Baal. There were 450 of them.

The people gathered around them. Elijah said, "You need to choose. Will you worship Baal or the one, true God. Two altars were built. When everything was ready for the sacrifice, Elijah said, "Pray to your god and I will pray to mine, and we will see which one sends down fire to light the offering."

The priests of Baal prayed and prayed all day long for the fire to come. They danced around their altar, but nothing happened. Elijah taunted them: "Shout louder! Maybe your god is thinking. Maybe he's just too busy. Perhaps he's on vacation. I know, maybe he's asleep and you need to wake him up!" The prophets of Baal shouted louder and louder, but still nothing happened.

Finally it was evening, and Elijah called the people to him. He placed twelve stones, one for each of the tribes of Israel, around God's altar. He dug a deep trench around the altar.

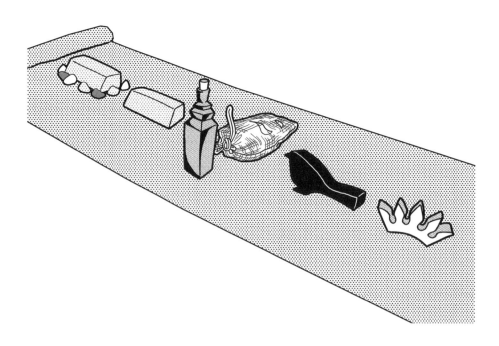

TWELVE STONES PLACED AROUND THE SECOND ALTAR (STORYTELLER'S PERSPECTIVE)

MOVEMENTS	WORDS
Wave your hand over it all to indicate the water.	He prepared the sacrifice, and when everything was ready, water was poured all over the altar. The trench was filled and overflowing. Then Elijah prayed to God. Fire fell from the heavens and burnt up the offering and dried up all the water. The people fell on their knees saying, "The Lord is God."
	It began to rain.
*Place **Object #6** (mountain from the top shelf) on the underlay.*	The king Ahab and his wife Jezebel were now even angrier with Elijah, so he had to run for his life and hide on the holy mountain of God. There he found a cave and went inside to sleep.
	In the night he thought he heard God calling to him. "What are you doing Elijah?" Elijah answered, "I have done everything you asked of me, but the people do not accept that you are the one, true God and they have killed your prophets. I am the only one left, and they are trying to kill me too." God said, "Go out and stand on the mountain. I will come to you."
As you mention the wind, earthquake and fire, make gentle movements with your hands over the mountain.	A powerful wind blew around the mountain, so strong that it smashed the rocks as it passed, but God was not in the wind. An earthquake shook the ground, shattering it. But God was not in the earthquake. A raging fire came and burned everything in its path. But God was not in the fire. Then there was sheer silence. When Elijah heard it, he wrapped his cape around him and stood at the mouth of the cave. He heard a still small voice and knew it was God. God told him to go back to the people, so he did. Ahab and Jezabel died, but he was a prophet in the land of Israel for the rest of his days.
*Place **Object #7** (painting or icon of Elijah and the chariot) on the underlay as you speak of Elijah going into heaven.*	When Elijah was about to die, he was with his friend Elisha. Elisha wanted to inherit a double share of the spirit of God that rested on Elijah. Elijah said, "If you see me as I am taken from you by God, then your request will be granted."

MOVEMENTS

WORDS

As they were speaking, it was as if a chariot of fire appeared, with horses made of fire, and the two men were separated. Elisha watched as Elijah was taken up into heaven in a whirlwind, and he knew God's spirit was with him and the people knew too. Elisha became a great prophet.

Sit for a moment and look at the lesson from beginning to end to let the story rest. Then begin the wondering.

I wonder what part of this story you liked the best?

I wonder what part was the most important?

I wonder what part was about you, or what part you were in?

I wonder if we could leave any of the story out and still have all the story that we need?

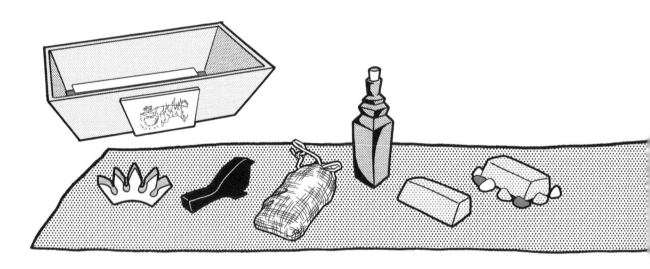

FINAL LAYOUT OF THE STORY OF THE PROPHET ELIJAH (CHILDREN'S PERSPECTIVE)

MOVEMENTS

After the wondering is over, show the children the control card for them to use to check their own telling of the story. Then put the story away carefully. Pick up each object in reverse order and remind the children what the object is, saying for example, "Here is one of the ravens that fed Elijah by the river...." After all of the objects are back in the tray, carefully model how to roll the underlay back up and place it in the tray as well. Return the lesson to its place on the shelf. Then return to your spot in the circle and dismiss the children one by one to their work.

WORDS

THE STORY OF THE PROPHET ISAIAH

LESSON NOTES

FOCUS: ISAIAH, A PROPHET OF DESTRUCTION AND OF HOPE (THE BOOK OF ISAIAH)

- ● SACRED STORY

- ● ENRICHMENT PRESENTATION

THE MATERIAL

- ● LOCATION: OLD TESTAMENT SACRED STORY SHELVES, BOTTOM SHELF, UNDER "ELIJAH"

- ● PIECES: MATCHES, 3 SMALL BASKETS (9 ″ X 5 ″) ON ONE LARGE TRAY (20 ″ X 14 ″):
  - — Basket #1 (Isaiah of Jerusalem): wood plaque with swirls of color/words and music of "Holy, Holy, Holy," coal, cluster of grapes, votive candle
  - — Basket #2: (Isaiah of the Exile): chain, strip of brown felt (identical to the pieces used to build the sheepfold in "The Parable of the Good Shepherd," *Volume 3,* p. 77), 1 of the People of God, rock, beautiful garment
  - — Basket # 3: (Third Isaiah): mother surrounded by children, scroll with words of Isaiah 61:1-4 printed on it, wolf and sheep (like what is used in the "Parable of the Good Shepherd," *Volume 3,* p. 77), material for "Creation," (*Volume 2,* p. 41")

- ● CONTROL

- ● UNDERLAY: DARK BROWN FELT STRIP, 57 ″ X 11 ″ (ONE LONG PIECE WITH STITCHING IN TWO PLACES TO MAKE IT LOOK AS THOUGH THE WHOLE THING IS REALLY THREE 19 ″ SCROLLS SEWN TOGETHER)

BACKGROUND

This presentation on Isaiah enriches the presentations on the Exile and Return (*Volume 2,* p. 93) and the Prophets (*Volume 2,* p. 100). The meditation of the 8th-century prophet Isaiah on the destiny of Jerusalem left a tradition of prophecy in his name. Chapters 1–29 of the book of Isaiah are now often called First Isaiah. This is a meditation on the crisis of pre-exilic Jerusalem in the years 742–701 B.C.E. Second Isaiah is in chapters 40–55. This takes place about 540 B.C.E. It tells of the hope for a return to Jerusalem from exile. Chapters 56–66 are called Third Isaiah. Its apparent context is after the return to and restoration of Jerusalem that was anticipated in Second Isaiah.

NOTES ON THE MATERIAL

Isaiah's story is actually three stories in one tray (20" x 14"). The three different stories are kept in three separate baskets (9" x 5") in a single tray. The story icon (5" x 2.5") is the wolf and the lamb from Isaiah 11:6 and 65:25. It can be attached to the end or the side of the tray depending on the size of the shelves, the classroom or other considerations. Each basket has its own story icon: First Isaiah has an image of Jerusalem attached, Second Isaiah has a piece of chain attached, and Third Isaiah has an image of the earth attached. The underlay is a strip of dark brown felt, 57" x 11". There is stitching at two places along the underlay (spaced about 19" apart) to make the underlay look as though it is three underlays stitched together. Each object in the story is approximately the same size (no more than 4" high and 4" wide).

First Isaiah, or "Isaiah of Jerusalem," calls for the following objects: a wooden plaque with swirls of color, some musical notation, and the words "Holy, Holy, Holy", a piece of wood painted to resemble a glowing coal, a cluster of grapes and a votive candle.

Second Isaiah, or "Isaiah of the Exile," calls for the following objects: a 10" piece of heavy chain, a strip of brown felt (like the pieces used to build the sheepfold in "The Parable of the Good Shepherd"), one of the People of God, a rock and a beautiful garment.

Third Isaiah, Isaiah of the "new creation," calls for the following objects: a small statue of a mother surrounded by children, a scroll with the words of the prophet in Isaiah 61:1-4, a wolf and a sheep (like what is used in "The Parable of the Good Shepherd") and materials for "Creation" (right from the top shelf).

A control for the lesson is folded and placed in the tray for the children to use to check their work. The sequence of the story is important because when you change the sequence, you change the story.

SPECIAL NOTES

The core stories about the People of God are placed on the top of the sacred story shelves. The enrichment stories about the key people in the core stories are placed on the lower shelves of the sacred story section in the room, under the core stories they enrich and extend (see diagram below).

Isaiah's story enriches the lesson on the Exile and Return (*Volume 2,* p. 93) and the Prophets (*Volume 2,* p. 100). When you introduce the stories in this volume, take care to set them in the larger context of the sacred story of which they are a part.

As you tell the story of Isaiah place objects on the underlay to remind you of each important event or prophecy. This time unroll the underlay all the way so the children can visually see that there are three sections from the start. At the end of the wondering, show the children the control card and then carefully place each object back in its basket and then in the tray saying something about each one like, "Here is the beautiful garment," and so forth. Lastly, model how to roll the underlay back up and place it in the tray.

STORY ICON FOR THE STORY OF THE PROPHET ISAIAH

STORY ICON FOR FIRST ISAIAH

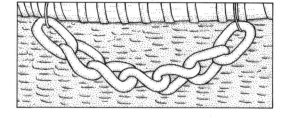

STORY ICON FOR SECOND ISAIAH

STORY ICON FOR THIRD ISAIAH

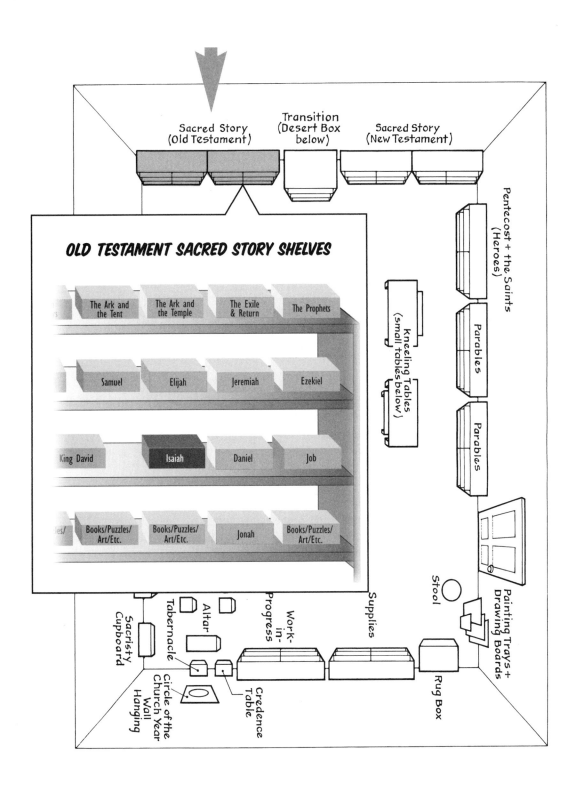

OLD TESTAMENT SACRED STORY SHELVES

WHERE TO FIND MATERIALS (TEACHING OBJECTS)

MOVEMENTS	WORDS
Move with deliberation to the shelf where the material waits.	Watch. Watch where I go.
Pick up the tray containing the material and return to the circle. (Be sure to have a container of matches such as from the "Baptism" lesson nearby so you can light the candle in this story.)	
Then go and get the "Creation" lesson from the top shelf. (You will need it for the end of the story.)	Oh...we need one more thing.
As you return to the circle you may need to say...	We need to be ready.
Take the underlay from the tray and unroll it all the way as you begin the introduction—from right to left (storyteller's perspective).	This is the story about the prophet Isaiah. But what is a prophet? Prophets are people who come so close to God and God comes so close to them that they know what God wants. Sometimes God's message is a warning for people who are not living in the best ways. Sometimes God has a message of hope for the people going through difficult times. Sometimes it is about making all things new.
As you mention the three scrolls, point out the places on the underlay where it has been stitched together...and as you mention the three baskets, place one at the beginning, and then the others at each of the places where the stitches can be seen between the underlay and the storyteller.	The words of Isaiah the prophet have been given to us written on a scroll. Some think there were three scrolls and that someone sewed them together. This is why we have three baskets.

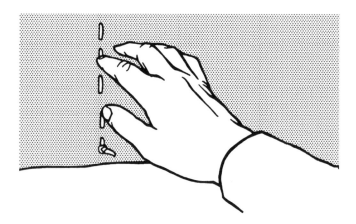

A PLACE ON THE UNDERLAY WHERE IT HAS BEEN STITCHED TOGETHER (STORYTELLER'S PERSPECTIVE)

MOVEMENTS

FIRST ISAIAH—ISAIAH OF JERUSALEM

*From Basket #1: Place **Object #1** (card with swirls of bright colors, musical notes and the words Holy, holy, holy") on the underlay as you say, "Holy, holy, holy."*

*Place **Object #2** (piece of wood painted to resemble glowing coal) on the underlay.*

*Place **Object #3** (bunch of grapes) on the underlay. Use your hand to draw the protective hedge and then cover the grapes. When you say that God removed the hedge, remove your hand.*

*Place **Object #4** (candle) on the underlay. Light the candle.*

WORDS

First Isaiah was called to be a prophet to the People of God during the time when the Assyrians were attacking the city. He had a vision. He suddenly found himself in the temple of God, but it was not like the temple in Jerusalem. It was even grander—a vision of heaven itself. Isaiah saw the Lord sitting upon a throne, high and lifted up; and his presence filled the temple. All around him were angels singing: "Holy, holy, holy is the Lord of hosts; the whole earth is full of God's glory."

Isaiah was afraid. He said, "I am just not good enough to be this close to God."

Just then an angel flew over to Isaiah and, taking a piece of burning coal from the altar, held it to Isaiah's lips, saying, "This has touched your lips and made you clean. Your sins are forgiven." Then Isaiah heard the Lord saying, "Whom shall I send to speak to the people? Who will go for us?" Isaiah said, "Here am I! Send me!"

Isaiah told the people that Jerusalem would be destroyed. He told how a lovely vineyard had been planted by God on a beautiful hill and surrounded it with a strong hedge. God thought the vineyard would grow good, sweet grapes, but instead it grew wild, bitter grapes. So God took away the hedge surrounding the vineyard, and the vines were trampled down. They became overgrown with briars and thorns. The rain did not fall on the ruined vineyard, so the vines withered and died.

Another time he told them about a light. Isaiah said, "The people who walked in darkness have seen a great light." But what was this light?

It was the brightness and warmth of a good harvest; of having a heavy load taken off your shoulders; of a child being born to show the way, a child called "Wonderful Counselor, Mighty God, Everlasting Father, Prince of Peace."

MOVEMENTS	WORDS

SECOND ISAIAH—THE PROPHET IN EXILE

From Basket #2: Place Object #1 (chain from "The Exile and Return") on the underlay as you speak about the exile.

Jerusalem was destroyed by the Babylonians and many of God's people were taken away to live in exile in Babylon.

Place Object #2: (felt cut to look like a straight road) on the underlay.

The exiles lived in a strange land, far from Jerusalem. One day Second Isaiah came to the people and said, "Get ready. Make straight in the desert a highway for our God. God is coming to be with you. God knows each one of you like a shepherd knows sheep. Do not be afraid."

Place Object #3 (one of the People of God) on the underlay.

Another time Second Isaiah came to the people and said someone is coming, someone who is chosen by God and in whom God delights. This one will teach people and refresh them when they are tired, but this person will be despised and rejected.

Place Object #4 (rock) on the underlay.

Still another time Second Isaiah told the people to remember all the way back to when the great family began and when they came through the water into freedom. When they remember and tell these stories, they will know who they are and where they came from. These stories will be like a statue that has been cut from a rock, to show them the way.

Place Object #5 (beautiful garment) on the underlay.

Finally, Second Isaiah told the People of God to get ready. They were going home, so they should prepare by making beautiful clothes to wear. When they put on those clothes, it would feel like they were already home.

MOVEMENTS

THIRD ISAIAH

From Basket #3: Place Object #1 (mother surrounded by children) on the underlay as you speak about the mother.

Place Object #2: (scroll) on the underlay.

Place Object #3 (wolf and sheep from "The Parable of the Good Shepherd") on the underlay.

Place Object #4 (creation story cards from "Creation") on the underlay.

WORDS

Some of the people did go home. The city of Jerusalem was rebuilt. God then sent more prophets to teach the people and fill them with hope for the future.

This was when Third Isaiah spoke. He said, "Lift up your eyes and look around, everyone is coming home. God will gather all the people of the world close—just as a mother does when she gathers her children close."

Another time Third Isaiah said to be at peace. It was hard to come back to Jerusalem. The city was all torn down and still black from the smoke and fire. God told Isaiah to tell the people that everything will be well.

Isaiah also said something like this: "The Spirit of the Lord God is upon me, because the Lord has anointed me to bring good tidings to the afflicted; he has sent me to bind up the brokenhearted, to proclaim liberty to the captives, and the opening of the prison to those who are bound; to proclaim the year of the Lord's favor, and the day of vengeance of our God; to comfort all who mourn; to grant to those who mourn in Zion—flowers instead of ashes, the oil of gladness instead of mourning, the mantle of praise instead of weakness; that they may be called oaks of righteousness, the planting of the Lord, that God may be glorified" (Isaiah 61:1-4).

God then told Isaiah to tell the people that some day the power of peace will be so strong that even enemies like wolves and lambs will eat together and be friends.

Third Isaiah said that God will make a new heaven and a new earth like he did so long ago at the beginning, but this time the new beginning will last forever.

MOVEMENTS

WORDS

COMPLETE LAYOUT OF THE STORY OF THE PROPHET ISAIAH (CHILDREN'S PERSPECTIVE)

Sit for a moment and look at the lesson from beginning to end to let the story rest. Then begin the wondering.

I wonder what part of this story you liked the best?

I wonder what part is the most important?

I wonder which part is about you or what part you are in?

I wonder if we could leave any of the story out and still have all that we need?

After the wondering is over, show the children the control card for them to use to check their own telling of the story. Then put the story away carefully. Pick up each object in reverse order and remind the children what the object is, saying for example, "Here is the wolf and the sheep..." After all of the objects are back in the tray, carefully model how to roll the underlay back up and place it in the tray as well. Return the lesson to its place on the shelf. Then return to your spot in the circle and dismiss the children one by one to their work.

THE STORY OF THE PROPHET JEREMIAH

LESSON NOTES

FOCUS: JEREMIAH, THE CHALLENGER OF FALSE PROPHETS (THE BOOK OF JEREMIAH)

- SACRED STORY
- ENRICHMENT PRESENTATION

THE MATERIAL

- LOCATION: OLD TESTAMENT SACRED STORY SHELVES, MIDDLE SHELF, UNDER "THE EXILE AND RETURN"
- PIECES: SHOFAR, LION AND WOLF, SUMMARY OF THE LAW (FROM "THE TEN BEST WAYS" VOLUME 2, P. 73), LINEN BELT, BROKEN PIECES OF CLAY POTTERY (IN SMALL BASKET OR OTHER CONTAINER), CUP FILLED WITH "POISON", PLATE OF NASTY FOOD, 10" PIECE OF CHAIN, PYRAMID, IMAGE OF RESTORED JERUSALEM
- CONTROL
- UNDERLAY: DARK BROWN FELT STRIP, 42" X 11"

BACKGROUND

The story of Jeremiah enriches the presentations on the Exile and Return (*Volume 2*, p. 93) and the Prophets (*Volume 2*, p. 100). Jeremiah was a major prophet during the decline and fall of the southern kingdom around Jerusalem (Judah). He lived during the time of the last five kings of Judah and was called to be a prophet around 627 B.C.E. when he was about 20 years old. He felt that the word of the Lord was "like a burning fire shut up in my bones" (Jeremiah 20:9). He lived through the invasion of Nebuchadnezzar who destroyed Jerusalem.

NOTES ON THE MATERIAL

Jeremiah's story sits in a deep wooden or wicker tray (12" x 8" x 3"). The story icon (5" x 2.5") is Jeremiah blowing a shofar. It can be attached to the end or the side of the tray. The underlay is a strip of dark brown felt, 42" x 11". Each object in the story is approximately the same size (no more than 4" high and 4" wide). The story calls for the following objects: a shofar, lion and wolf, the Summary of the Law (from "The Ten Best Ways"), a linen belt, broken pieces of clay pottery, a plate of nasty food, a cup filled with poison (grey glue works well), a 10" piece of chain, a pyramid and an image of Jerusalem restored.

A control for the lesson is folded and placed in the tray for the children to use to check their work. The sequence of the story is important because when you change the sequence, you change the story.

SPECIAL NOTES

The core stories about the People of God are placed on the top of the sacred story shelves. The enrichment stories about the key people in the core stories are placed on the lower shelves of the sacred story section in the room, under the core stories they enrich and extend (see diagram below).

This lesson on Jeremiah enriches the lessons on the Exile and Return (*Volume 2*, p. 93) and the Prophets (*Volume 2,* p. 100).When you introduce the stories in this volume, take care to set them in the larger context of the sacred story of which they are a part.

As you tell the story of Jeremiah, place objects on the underlay to remind you of each important event or prophecy. Unroll the underlay slowly, just enough for each object, as if you are unrolling a life. At the end of the wondering, show the children the control card, then carefully place each object back in the tray saying something about each event like, "Here is the linen belt God told Jeremiah to bury in the ground," and so forth. Lastly, model how to roll the underlay back up and place it in the tray.

STORY ICON FOR THE STORY OF THE PROPHET JEREMIAH

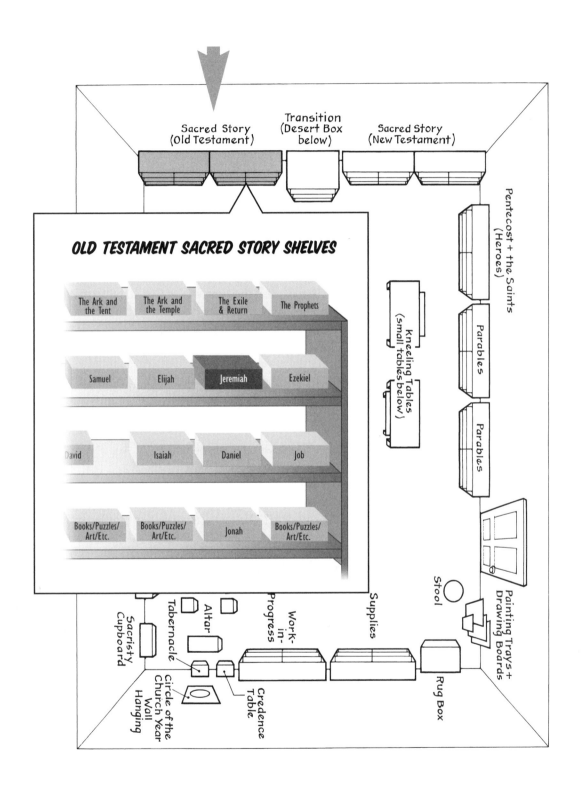

OLD TESTAMENT SACRED STORY SHELVES

Sacred Story (Old Testament)

Transition (Desert Box below)

Sacred Story (New Testament)

| The Ark and the Tent | The Ark and the Temple | The Exile & Return | The Prophets |

| Samuel | Elijah | Jeremiah | Ezekiel |

| David | Isaiah | Daniel | Job |

| Books/Puzzles/ Art/Etc. | Books/Puzzles/ Art/Etc. | Jonah | Books/Puzzles/ Art/Etc. |

Pentecost + the Saints (Heroes)

Kneeling Tables (small tables below)

Parables

Parables

Stool

Painting Trays + Drawing Boards

Rug Box

Supplies

Work-in-Progress

Credence Table

Circle of the Church Year Wall Hanging

Altar

Tabernacle

Sacristy Cupboard

WHERE TO FIND MATERIALS (TEACHING OBJECTS)

MOVEMENTS	**WORDS**
Move with deliberation to the shelf where the material waits.	Watch. Watch where I go.
Pick up Jeremiah's tray and return to the circle.	
As you return to the circle you may need to say...	We need to be ready.
Remove the underlay from the tray and unroll it—just enough to place the first object—right to left (storyteller's perspective).	This is the story of the prophet Jeremiah. But what is a prophet?

Prophets are people who come so close to God and God comes so close to them that they know what God wants. Sometimes people do not like the message, so they become very angry with the prophet. It's not easy being a prophet.

Jeremiah lived in the great city of Jerusalem after the Assyrian army had come and gone. God said, "I will make you a prophet to the nations." Jeremiah was worried, because he was still so young.

God said, "Don't worry. I will be with you." |
*Place **Object #1** (shofar) on the underlay.*	One day Jeremiah went all around inside and outside the city walls blowing a trumpet. The people asked him, "Why are you blowing a trumpet?" He said, "You have gone too far away from God. It is time to come back. God says, 'I am the one who led you through the water into freedom and across the desert. I gave you the Ten Best Ways to live. I am your God. You are my people. Come back!'"
*Place **Object #2** (lion and Wolf) on the underlay.*	God showed Jeremiah things that would happen in Jerusalem, things so frightening that even hearing about them would make the ears of the people tingle. Jeremiah was afraid. But he did what God told him to do. He said, "A nation will come and attack us like a lion and destroy us like a wolf," but the people would not listen.
*Place **Object #3** (Summary of the Law) on the underlay.*	Another time Jeremiah went into the temple. He said to the people there, "Pay attention! Remember the Ten Commandments. Love God and love people. Stop worshipping other gods. God says, 'Turn around. Change your ways, or I will tear down the temple,'" but still the people would not listen.

MOVEMENTS	WORDS
Place **Object #4** (linen belt) on the underlay.	Once God told Jeremiah to buy a linen belt and put it around his waist. Then God told him to take it off and hide it in some rocks. Many days later God told him to go back and get it, but now it was ruined and completely useless. God said, "The people are like this belt. They refuse to listen to my words and are now completely useless!"
Place **Object #5** (broken pieces of clay pottery in a pouch) on the underlay when you speak of breaking the jar.	Another day God told Jeremiah to go buy a clay jar from a potter and take it to the Valley of Ben Hinmon. There in the presence of the people he broke the jar and said, "God says, 'I will smash this nation and this city just as this potter's jar is smashed and cannot be repaired.'" Jeremiah's words made the people very angry—so angry that they put his hands and feet into pieces of wood called stocks and left him there overnight. Many more times they put him in prison. They did not want to listen.
Place **Object #6** (cup filled with "poison" and plate of nasty food) on the underlay as you speak of the false prophets' drinking poison and eating bitter food.	While Jeremiah was prophesying, there were false prophets throughout the country. A false prophet is someone who only pretends to speak for God. They did not tell the people the truth. The false prophets God very sad and angry.

God told Jeremiah to tell the people that God would punish the false prophets. They will eat bitter food and drink poisoned water. God told Jeremiah to warn the people not to listen to them. |
| Place **Object #7** (chain) on the underlay when you say, "They were in exile." | Jeremiah hod told the truth. The Babylonians did come and destroy the city. They took the king and many of the best people to Babylon. They were in exile. They could not go home. |
| Place **Object #8** (pyramid) on the underlay. | The people remaining in Jerusalem were frightened. They did not want to be taken into exile, so they decided to run away. They went to Egypt and asked Jeremiah if this was the right thing to do. Jeremiah asked God.

God said, "No. They should not go to Egypt." God promised that the people would be cared for. Once again they refused to listen, so they went to Egypt anyway. They even forced Jeremiah to go with them. |
| Place **Object #9** (image of a restored Jerusalem) on the underlay. | Even as the city of Jerusalem lay in ruins, God spoke words of hope and consolation through Jeremiah, and they were written down and kept for us to read. |

MOVEMENTS

WORDS

"I will bring health and healing to the city. I will heal my people and give them peace. I will bring the people back from exile and will rebuild the city as before. I will forgive them all their sins. A new king will be born—one who will do what is just and right in the land."

Sit for a moment and look at the lesson from beginning to end to let the story rest. Then begin the wondering.

I wonder what part of this story you liked the best?

I wonder what part was the most important?

I wonder what part was about you, or what part you were in?

I wonder if we could leave any of the story out and still have all the story that we need?

FINAL LAYOUT OF THE STORY OF THE PROPHET JEREMIAH (CHILDREN'S PERSPECTIVE)

MOVEMENTS

After the wondering is over, show the children the control card for them to use to check their own telling of the story. Then put the story away carefully. Pick up each object in reverse order and remind the children what the object is, saying for example, "Here are the pieces of pottery left after Jeremiah broke the clay pot..." After all of the objects are back in the tray, carefully model how to roll the underlay back up and place it in the tray as well. Return the lesson to its place on the shelf. Then return to your spot in the circle and dismiss the children one by one to their work.

WORDS

THE STORY OF THE PROPHET EZEKIEL

LESSON NOTES

FOCUS: EZEKIEL, A PROPHET TO THE EXILES (THE BOOK OF EZEKIEL)

- SACRED STORY
- ENRICHMENT PRESENTATION

THE MATERIAL

- LOCATION: OLD TESTAMENT SACRED STORY SHELVES, MIDDLE SHELF, BESIDE JEREMIAH
- PIECES: 10" CHAIN, IMAGE OF EZEKIEL'S VISION OF GOD (THE WHEEL, ETC.) MOUNTED ON WOOD, SCROLL, BRICK, GOOD SHEPHERD AND ORDINARY SHEPHERD (IDENTICAL TO THOSE IN "THE PARABLE OF THE GOOD SHEPHERD," VOLUME 3, P. 77), SMALL PITCHER, COLLECTION OF "DRY" BONES, PICTURE OF JERUSALEM RESTORED
- CONTROL
- UNDERLAY: DARK BROWN FELT STRIP, 42" X 11"

BACKGROUND

The story of Ezekiel enriches the presentations on the Exile and Return (*Volume 2*, p. 93) and the Prophets (*Volume 2*, p. 100). Ezekiel was deported from Jerusalem in 598 with some 10,000 elite of the city. He was a contemporary of Jeremiah, but his call to be a prophet came on the banks of the Chebar in Babylon (Ezekiel 1:1). With the exception of 1:2-3, this book is almost completely made up of his personal visions. They were shared with others and written down in his own house.

NOTES ON THE MATERIAL

Ezekiel's story sits in a deep wooden or wicker tray (12" x 8" x 3"). The story icon (5" x 2.5") is an image of Ezekiel's vision, a "wheel within a wheel." It can be attached to the end or the side of the tray depending on the size of the shelves, the classroom or other considerations. The underlay is a strip of dark brown felt, 42" x 11". Each object in the story is approximately the same size (no more than 4" high and 4" wide). The story calls for the following objects: a 10" piece of chain, an image of Ezekiel's Vision of God (the wheel, etc.), a scroll, a brick, a Good Shepherd and an ordinary shepherd (just like what is used in the Parable of the Good Shepherd), a small pitcher, a collection "dry bones" and a picture of Jerusalem restored.

A control for the lesson is folded and placed in the tray for the children to use to check their work. The sequence of the story is important because when you change the sequence, you change the story.

SPECIAL NOTES

The core stories about the People of God are placed on the top of the sacred story shelves. The enrichment stories about the key people in the core stories are placed on the lower shelves of the sacred story section in the room, under the core stories they enrich and extend (see diagram below).

This lesson on Ezekiel enriches the lesson on the Exile and Return (*Volume 2*, p. 93) and the Prophets (*Volume 2,* p. 100). When you introduce the stories in this volume, take care to set them in the larger context of the sacred story of which they are a part.

As you tell the story of Ezekiel and his prophetic visions, place objects on the underlay to remind you of each important prophetic vision. Unroll the underlay slowly, just enough for each object, as if you are unrolling a life. At the end of the wondering, show the children the control card and carefully place each object back in the tray saying something about each event like, "Here is the Good Shepherd and the Ordinary Shepherd," and so forth. Lastly, model how to roll the underlay back up and place it in the tray.

STORY ICON FOR THE STORY OF THE PROPHET EZEKIEL

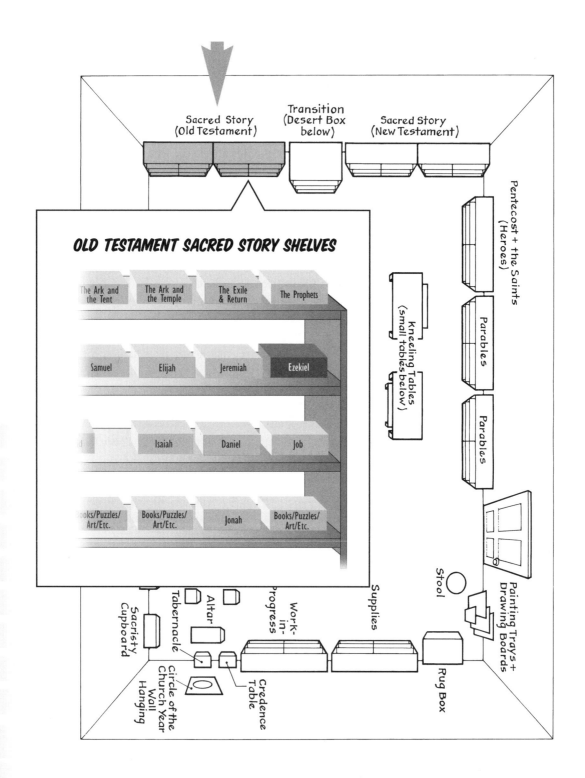

OLD TESTAMENT SACRED STORY SHELVES

Sacred Story (Old Testament)

Transition (Desert Box below)

Sacred Story (New Testament)

The Ark and the Tent

The Ark and the Temple

The Exile & Return

The Prophets

Samuel

Elijah

Jeremiah

Ezekiel

Isaiah

Daniel

Job

Books/Puzzles/Art/Etc.

Books/Puzzles/Art/Etc.

Jonah

Books/Puzzles/Art/Etc.

Pentecost + the Saints (Heroes)

Parables

Parables

Kneeling Tables (small tables below)

Painting Trays + Drawing Boards

Stool

Rug Box

Supplies

Work-in-progress

Sacristy Cupboard

Tabernacle

Altar

Circle of the Church Year Wall Hanging

Credence Table

WHERE TO FIND MATERIALS (TEACHING OBJECTS)

MOVEMENTS	WORDS
Move with deliberation to the shelf where the material waits.	Watch. Watch where I go.
Pick up Ezekiel's tray and return to the circle.	
As you return to the circle you may need to say...	We need to be ready.
Remove the underlay from the tray and begin to unroll—just enough to place the first object—right to left (storyteller's perspective).	This is the story of the prophet Ezekiel's visions. But what is a prophet?

Prophets are people who come so close to God and God comes so close to them that they know what God wants. |
| *Place **Object 1** (chain) on the underlay when you say the word* exile. | Ezekiel was a prophet to the people in exile in Babylon. The exiles would gather by the river to worship God. They didn't know if God would find them in that strange land, so they often faced toward Jerusalem and the temple, where they knew God was. |
| *Place **Object #2** (painting or drawing of Ezekiel's vision) on the underlay.* | One day while gathered at the river with the other exiles, Ezekiel had a vision. He saw a storm coming. In the clouds were four living creatures. They looked like men but had wings. Each one had four different faces—all of different animals. When they moved their wings it sounded like thunder.

Each creature had a wheel within a wheel. The wheels seemed almost alive. When Ezekiel looked up, he saw God sitting on a throne, being carried by these four creatures. Ezekiel was afraid and fell to the ground. |
| *Place **Object #3** (scroll) on the underlay as you mention the scroll.* | God spoke to Ezekiel saying, "Son of man, stand upon your feet, and I will speak with you." And the Spirit of God entered Ezekiel and lifted him up onto his feet. And God said, "Son of man, eat what I give to you; eat this scroll, so that my words may live in you." And Ezekiel ate the scroll and found it to be sweet like honey.

This vision was only the first one he had. Before his time as a prophet was over, he had about fifty more visions. At first most of the messages Ezekiel brought to the exiles were about the coming destruction of Jerusalem. Later they were about hope for God's people. |

MOVEMENTS	WORDS
*Place **Object #4** (brick) on the underlay.*	One time God told Ezekiel to take a brick while it was still wet and draw a map of Jerusalem on it. Then he put the brick on the ground so everyone could see and he put a toy army around it ready to take over the city. Ezekiel did this to show that Jerusalem would be destroyed by the Babylonians. There were many more prophecies of the destruction of Jerusalem and its temple, and all of them came true. The city crumbled—there was little left.
*Place **Object #5** (Good Shepherd and ordinary shepherd) on the underlay.*	After Jerusalem was destroyed God began to send messages of hope to his people through his prophet Ezekiel. One of them was about a shepherd. Ezekiel told the people that sometimes shepherds are not like the Good Shepherd. They are not even like the ordinary shepherd. They are bad. But God will come and rescue the people from the bad shepherds. God says, "I myself will be the shepherd of the people and will bring them into their own land."
*Place **Object #6** (clear, glass pitcher) on the underlay.*	One day another message of hope came to Ezekiel. He told the people that God will sprinkle clean water upon them when he brings them home to Jerusalem to cleanse them from all their wrongdoings. "A new heart I will give you," says God, "and a new spirit I will put with you. You will be my people, and I will be your God."

MOVEMENTS

*Pour **Object #7** (bones) onto the underlay as you speak of them.*

*Place **Object #8** (picture of Jerusalem restored) on the underlay.*

Sit for a moment and look at the lesson from beginning to end to let the story rest. Then begin the wondering.

After the wondering is over, show the children the control card for them to use to check their own telling of the story. Then put the story away carefully. Pick up each object in reverse order and remind the children what the object is, saying for example, "Here are the dry bones that came to life..." After all of the objects are back in the tray, carefully model how to roll the underlay back up and place it in the tray as well. Return the lesson to its place on the shelf. Then return to your spot in the circle and dismiss the children one by one to their work.

WORDS

Yet another time God showed Ezekiel a pile of dry bones. God breathed new life into them and they became alive, like God's people were going to come alive. God said, "I will put my Spirit in them and they will live."

Ezekiel died in exile. He had witnessed the loss and destruction of his beloved city, but he also saw a beautiful vision of a people living in a restored city who were content. The city would be called *The Lord is there.*

I wonder what part of this story you liked the best?

I wonder what part was the most important?

I wonder what part was about you, or what part you were in?

I wonder if we could leave any of the story out and still have all the story that we need?

COMPLETE LAYOUT OF THE STORY OF THE PROPHET EZEKIEL (CHILDREN'S PERSPECTIVE)

THE STORY OF DANIEL

LESSON NOTES

FOCUS: DANIEL, HERO AND VISIONARY OF END TIMES (THE BOOK OF DANIEL)

- SACRED STORY
- ENRICHMENT PRESENTATION

THE MATERIAL

- LOCATION: OLD TESTAMENT SACRED STORY SHELVES, MIDDLE SHELF, UNDER "THE PROPHETS"
- PIECES: 10" CHAIN, PAINTING OF A GOLDEN FIGURE MOUNTED ON A WOODEN PLAQUE (SEE DANIEL 2:31FF), GOLDEN STATUE, PAINTING OF A GREAT TREE COVERED WITH FRUIT AND SURROUNDED BY ANIMALS OF ALL KINDS MOUNTED ON A WOODEN PLAQUE, WOODEN PLAQUE PAINTED TO LOOK LIKE A GREY STONE WALL WITH THE WORDS MENE, MENE, TEKEL, PARSIN WRITTEN IN HEBREW ON IT, LION'S DEN, PAINTINGS OF DANIEL'S 4 VISIONS (THE 4 BEASTS IN DANIEL 7:1-8, THE RAM AND THE HE-GOAT IN DANIEL 8:1-10, GABRIEL IN DANIEL 9:20-27, THE MAN CLOTHED IN LINEN IN DANIEL 10:5-7)
- CONTROL
- UNDERLAY: THIS UNDERLAY IS UNIQUE IN THAT IT HAS TWO SECTIONS. THE FIRST SECTION IS DARK BROWN FELT (35" X 11") AND THE SECOND SECTION IS MULTI-COLORED CLOTH (29" X 11").

BACKGROUND

This lesson enriches both the lesson called Exile and Return (*Volume 2*, p. 93) and the lesson on the Prophets (*Volume 2*, p. 100). The despair that denies its own reality is impossible to cope with directly. Teaching "facts," biblical or otherwise, cannot accomplish the transformation of despair to hope, when all the facts conspire to reinforce the unacknowledged despair.

The hero stories of chapters 1–6 in Daniel and the apocalyptic visions of chapter 7–12 are ways to indirectly and symbolically present a whole new system of meaning to provide permission for the repressed despair to be named and the false goals of society to be challenged by a bright vision of the future.

"Pie in the sky" and other utopian schemes, religious or secular, will not touch such despair, but hero stories about being true to one's deepest values despite the unworthy values promoted by political leadership and visions of a hopeful future might.

If you don't think children are susceptible to such despair as that addressed by the Book of Daniel, you need to work for a few years with families who have suicidal children.

NOTES ON THE MATERIAL

Daniel's story sits on a deep wooden or wicker tray (12" x 8" x 3"). The story icon (5" x 2.5") is Daniel in the lion's den. It can be attached to the end or the side of the tray depending on the size of the shelves, the classroom or other considerations. The underlay is unique in that it is in two sections. The first section is dark brown felt (35" x 11"), and the second section is multi-colored cloth (29" x 11"). The first section is about Daniel's interactions with a king and his court; the second section is about Daniel's prophetic visions. Each object in the story is approximately the same size (no more than 4" high and 4" wide). The story calls for the following objects and images: a 10" piece of chain, a painting of a golden figure mounted on a wooden plaque (see Daniel 2:31ff), a golden statue, a painting of a great tree covered with fruit and surrounded by animals of all kinds mounted on a wooden plaque, a wooden plaque painted to look like a grey stone wall with the words *Mene, Mene, Tekel, Parsin* written in Hebrew on it, the lion's den, paintings of Daniel's four visions (the four beasts from Daniel 7:1-8, the ram and the he-goat from Daniel 8:1-10, Gabriel from Daniel 9:20-27, and the man clothed in linen from Daniel 10:5-7).

A control for the lesson is folded and placed in the tray for the children to use to check their work. The sequence of the story is important because when you change the sequence, you change the story.

SPECIAL NOTES

The core stories about the People of God are placed on the top of the sacred story shelves. The enrichment stories about the key people in the core stories are placed on the lower shelves of the sacred story section in the room, under the core stories they enrich and extend (see diagram below).

This lesson enriches both the lesson called Exile and Return (*Volume 2*, p. 93) and the lesson on the Prophets (*Volume 2*, p. 100). When you introduce the stories in this volume, take care to set them in the larger context of the sacred story of which they are a part. You can accomplish this by:
• presenting the top shelf story the week before and then following up with this,
• presenting the top shelf story briefly on the same day you present this, or
• standing by the shelf and reminding the children of the top shelf story before bringing this one to the circle.

As you tell the story of Daniel place objects on the underlay to remind you of each important event, a prophecy, or a vision. Unroll the underlay slowly, just enough for each object, as if you are unrolling a life. At the end of the wondering, carefully place each object back in the tray saying something about each event like, "Here is Daniel's vision of the four beasts," and so forth. Lastly, model how to roll the underlay back up and place it in the tray.

STORY ICON FOR THE STORY OF DANIEL

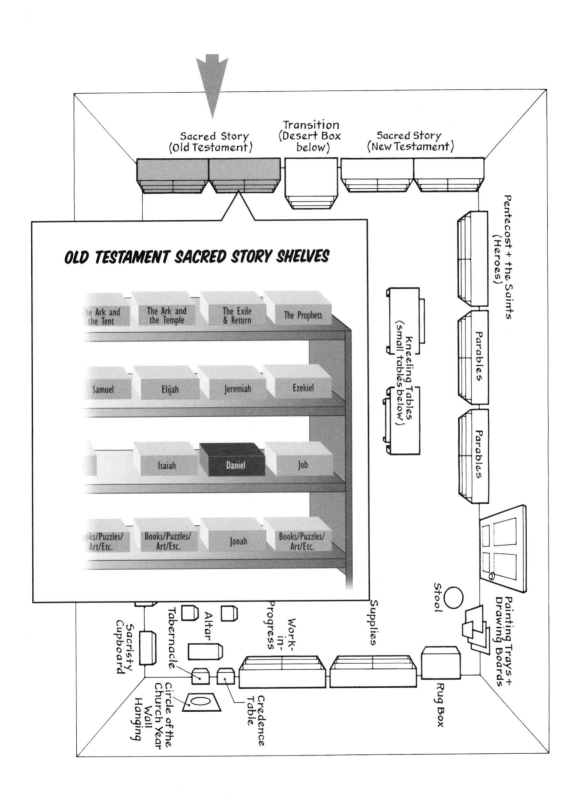

OLD TESTAMENT SACRED STORY SHELVES

Sacred Story
(Old Testament)

Transition
(Desert Box
below)

Sacred Story
(New Testament)

Pentecost + the Saints
(Heroes)

Parables

Parables

Kneeling Tables
(small tables below)

The Ark and
the Tent

The Ark and
the Temple

The Exile
& Return

The Prophets

Samuel

Elijah

Jeremiah

Ezekiel

Isaiah

Daniel

Job

Books/Puzzles/
Art/Etc.

Books/Puzzles/
Art/Etc.

Jonah

Books/Puzzles/
Art/Etc.

Painting Trays +
Drawing Boards

Stool

Rug Box

Supplies

Work-
in-
Progress

Credence
Table

Tabernacle

Altar

Sacristy
Cupboard

Circle of the
Church Year
Wall
Hanging

WHERE TO FIND MATERIALS (TEACHING OBJECTS)

MOVEMENTS	WORDS
Move with deliberation to the shelf where the material waits.	⇒ Watch. Watch where I go.
Pick up Daniel's tray and return to the circle.	
As you return to the circle you may need to say...	⇒ We need to be ready.
Take the underlay off of the tray and begin to unroll it—just enough to place the first object—right to left (storyteller's perspective).	
*Place **Object #1** (chain) on the underlay when you say the word* exile.	⇒ The people were in exile. They had been living in Babylon for a long time, so many had gotten used to living there. Some even had jobs in the court of the king. Daniel and his three friends, Shadrach, Meshach and Abednego, worked at the king's court. God blessed Daniel and his friends with learning, wisdom and skill.
*Place **Object #2** (painting of the great shining figure) on the underlay.*	⇒ One day the king of Babylon had a dream. He saw a great shining figure. As he watched it fell apart and blew away in the wind. None of the king's wise men knew what it meant, but Daniel did. A time will come when all the kingdoms of the world will be destroyed. But God's kingdom will last forever.
*Place **Object #3** (golden statue) on the underlay.*	⇒ Another day the king made a huge gold statue of a person. He commanded the people to bow down when they heard special music and worship the image. The people who did not obey would be thrown into a furnace full of fire. Daniel's friends, Shadrach, Meshach and Abednego would not worship the statue, so they were thrown into the blazing furnace. God sent an angel to keep them safe, and not a hair on their heads was burned in the fire. The king was amazed, so he gave the three friends a place of honor in his court.

MOVEMENTS

*Place **Object #4** (painting of a great tree) on the underlay.*

*Place **Object #5** (wooden plaque with the words* Mene, Mene, Tekel, Parsin *written on it) on the underlay.*

*Place **Object #6** (lion's den) on the underlay.*

WORDS

The king had another dream. The wise men of the court could not understand it, so they brought Daniel to the king again. The king dreamed about a tree that touched the sky. It had beautiful leaves and fruit. Animals found shelter under it and its branches were full of birds. The Holy One came down from heaven and said, "Cut down the tree and let the animals flee and the birds fly away."

Daniel prayed to God and God showed him what it meant. Daniel told the king, "The tree you saw was you. You are great and strong like the tree, but you will be driven away from your people and live like an animal, eating grass, for seven long years."

And the dream was true. The king was driven out and lived like and animal for seven years. When he came back to his throne he worshipped the one, true God.

After the king died, his son began to rule. He did not know the one, true God. One time he held a great feast and used the holy things from the temple in Jerusalem that the Babylonians had brought to their own city.

Suddenly the people at the party saw the fingers of a human hand writing on the wall. The king could not read the writing, so he sent for Daniel. The words were *Mene, Mene, Tekel, Parsin,* which meant, "God will bring this king's rule to an end, and the kingdom of Babylon will be divided and given to the Medes and Persians."

That very night the king was killed and King Darius took over.

King Darius divided his new kingdom into 120 parts and placed three rulers over them. One of these three was Daniel.

The other two rulers were jealous of Daniel. They knew he was the king's favorite and might one day rule over them. They decided to trick the king into making a law that Daniel could not keep. Everyone had to pray only to King Darius or be cast into a den of lions. They knew that Daniel worshipped the one, true God, so he would never pray to a king.

MOVEMENTS	WORDS
	One day Daniel was caught in his room, facing Jerusalem, and praying to God. They brought him to the king. The king liked Daniel, but a law was a law. Daniel was thrown into the den of lions.
	The king worried about Daniel. In the morning he ran to the lion's den and called to Daniel. Daniel answered, "I am fine! God sent an angel to protect me from the lions." The king was filled with gladness and he gave orders to lift Daniel out of the den. Then the men who had accused Daniel were thrown into the lion's den instead and all were killed.
	Daniel was honored throughout the kingdom, and he prospered all the rest of his life.
Change the underlay from brown felt to multi-colored cloth.	Daniel also had visions and dreams himself.
*Place **Vision 1** (painting of fur beasts) on the underlay.*	One time Daniel dreamed that four great beasts came up out of the sea. The first was like a lion and had eagle's wings. The second looked like a bear standing on its hind legs with three ribs in its mouth. The third was like a leopard but had four wings on its back and four heads. The last beast was more terrifying than the rest and very strong. It had great iron teeth and ten horns.

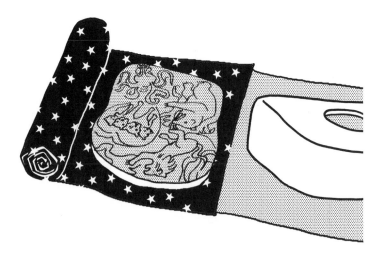

FOUR BEASTS ON THE MULTI-COLORED CLOTH (STORYTELLER'S PERSPECTIVE)

MOVEMENTS	WORDS
	As he looked another horn appeared that rooted out three of the horns. As Daniel watched, this fourth beast was put to death. The others were not killed, but they lost all their powers. Then God appeared and ruled the rest forever.
	Daniel woke from his dream very troubled. He told his helper about all that he had seen. His helper told Daniel what it meant. He said, "Four kings will rise out of the earth. But their power will not last. It is God alone who will rule forever."
*Place **Vision 2** (painting of ram and goat) on the underlay.*	Another time Daniel had a vision of himself standing by a river. Beside him was a ram with two horns, one longer than the other. This ram charged all around destroying everything in its path, and as it charged it became stronger. As Daniel watched, a male goat appeared from the West. It was as if it were flying. The goat had a horn between its eyes. The goat charged the ram, breaking its two horns and trampling it on the ground.
	Daniel could not understand what he saw. But an angel named Gabriel came to him and told him that this was a vision of the end of all time. A king will arise, more powerful and evil than all the others. This dream frightened Daniel.
	Daniel prayed for many days, asking the Lord to forgive the people for their evil ways and to restore the great city of Jerusalem. Daniel remembered that the prophet Jeremiah had said that the city would be restored after seventy years, and yet it remained in pieces.
*Place **Vision 3** (angel Gabriel) on the underlay.*	One day as he prayed the angel Gabriel appeared to him again.
	Gabriel said, "The Lord God has heard your prayers and has sent me to try and help you understand." Jeremiah meant seventy times seven—a much longer time than anyone imagined. This was because the sin of the people was so great.
	The words of the angel Gabriel filled Daniel with great sadness. He fasted for three weeks and then God sent him another vision.

MOVEMENTS

Place **Vision 4** *(man dressed in linen) on the underlay.*

Sit for a moment and look at the les-son from beginning to end to let the story rest. Then begin the wondering.

WORDS

This time Daniel saw someone like a man dressed in linen with a belt of gold around his waist. Daniel fell to the ground before him. A hand touched him and raised him up. The figure like a man said to Daniel, "Do not be afraid. Be strong and courageous! I have come to help you understand these visions." He told Daniel that the power of all kings will come to an end. He ex-plained that this time will be difficult, but that God will stay close to God's people and deliver them from all danger. They will live with God forever.

Then the figure like a man told Daniel to keep all these things secret. And he promised Daniel that all would be well for him and all of God's people.

I wonder what part of this whole story you liked the best?

I wonder what part is the most important?

I wonder what part is about you, or what part you are in?

I wonder if we could leave any of the story out and still have all that we need?

COMPLETE LAYOUT OF THE STORY OF DANIEL (CHILDREN'S PERSPECTIVE)

MOVEMENTS

After the wondering is over, put the story away carefully. Pick up each object in reverse order and remind the children what the object is, saying for example, "Here are the visions Daniel had..." After all of the objects are back in the tray, carefully model how to roll the underlay back up and place it in the tray as well. Return the lesson to its place on the shelf. Then return to your spot in the circle and dismiss the children one by one to their work.

WORDS

THE STORY OF JOB

LESSON NOTES

FOCUS: WISDOM ABOUT THE DEPTHS OF FAITH AND SUFFERING (THE BOOK OF JOB)

- SACRED STORY
- ENRICHMENT STORY

THE MATERIAL

- LOCATION: OLD TESTAMENT SACRED STORY SHELVES, BOTTOM SHELF, UNDER "DANIEL"
- PIECES: 2 6" SQUARES OF GREEN FELT, 1 6" SQUARE OF BROWN FELT, 1 6" SQUARE OF GREY FELT, 18 PEOPLE OF GOD (JOB, MRS. JOB, JOB'S 7 CHILDREN, 5 NEW CHILDREN, JOB'S 4 FRIENDS), PLASTIC CAMEL, SHEEP AND COW, WHIRLWIND (CLAY SHAPED TO LOOK LIKE A TORNADO OR FUNNEL CLOUD), FISH HOOK, 10" PIECE OF FISHING LINE
- CONTROL
- UNDERLAY: DARK BROWN FELT STRIP, 42" X 11"

BACKGROUND

Job is linked in general to the search of the people of God for the mystery of the presence of God. It is a kind of commentary on the whole journey. Jewish tradition recognizes three kinds of literature in the Jewish scriptures: *the law* (including its stories), *the prophets* and *the writings*. Job is from the writings. Among the writings are psalms, poetry, visions and other kinds of literature. Job is unique. It is a folktale layered with levels of literary meaning about God's presence despite our inability to understand that presence.

NOTES ON THE MATERIAL

Job's story sits on a deep wooden or wicker tray (12" x 8" x 3"). The story icon (5" x 2.5") is a whirlwind. It can be attached to the end or the side of the tray depending on the size of the shelves, the classroom or other considerations. The underlay is a strip of dark brown felt, 42" x 11". Each object in the story is approximately the same size (no more than 4" high and 4" wide). The story calls for the following objects: two 6" squares of green felt, one 6" square of brown felt, one 6" square of grey felt, 18 People of God (Job, Mrs. Job, Job's seven children, five new children and Job's four friends), a camel, sheep and cow, a whirlwind, a fish hook, and a 10" length of fishing line.

A control for the lesson is folded and placed in the tray for the children to use to check their work. The sequence of the story is important because when you change the sequence, you change the story.

SPECIAL NOTES

The core stories about the People of God are placed on the top of the sacred story shelves. The enrichment stories about the key people in the core stories are placed on the lower shelves of the sacred story section in the room, under the core stories they enrich and extend (see diagram below).

When you introduce the stories in this volume, take care to set them in the larger context of the sacred story of which they are a part. You can accomplish this by:
- presenting the top shelf story the week before and then following up with this,
- presenting the top shelf story briefly on the same day you present this, or
- standing by the shelf and reminding the children of the top shelf story before bringing this one to the circle.

As you tell the story of his life place objects on the underlay to remind you of each important event. Unroll the underlay slowly, just enough for each object, as if you are unrolling a timeline. At the end of the wondering, carefully place each object back in the tray saying something about each event like, "Here are Job's friends," and so forth. Lastly, model how to roll the underlay back up and place it in the tray.

STORY ICON FOR THE STORY OF JOB

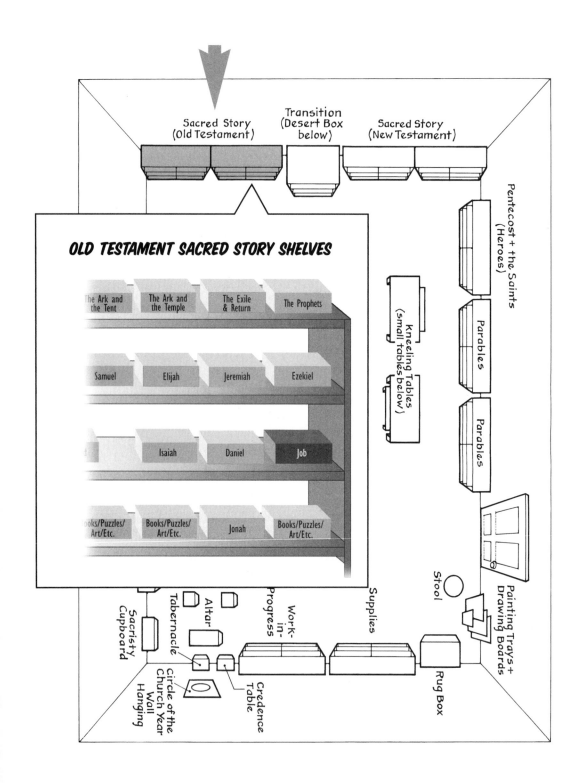

WHERE TO FIND MATERIALS (TEACHING OBJECTS)

MOVEMENTS

Move with deliberation to the shelf where the material waits.

Pick up Job's tray and return to the circle.

As you return to the circle you may need to say...

Take the underlay from the tray and begin to unroll the underlay—just enough to place the first object—right to left (from the storyteller's perspective).

Object #1: *As you tell the story, place the green felt square on the brown underlay and place Job on the underlay. Place the sheep, cow, camel, Job's wife and children all around him.*

WORDS

▧ Watch. Watch where I go.

▧ We need to be ready.

▧ There was once a man who lived in the land of Uz. He had many sheep and all kinds of animals. He had a large family and loved them very much.

SHEEP, COW, CAMEL, JOB'S WIFE AND CHILDREN AROUND JOB (STORYTELLER'S PERSPECTIVE)

MOVEMENTS

Sweep your hand above the scene you've made to suggest that God and Satan are above, looking at the family.

Object #2: Place the brown square beside the green one on the underlay. Move Job and Mrs. Job to this new spot, leaving behind everything else.

Object #3: Move Job to the grey square. Place his three friends around him.

WORDS

One day God said to Satan, "Have you seen Job? He is truly good."

Satan said, "No he's not. It is easy to be good when you have so much.

God said, "But he is good."

Satan said, "Let's see."

God said, "Do what you will."

Job sat in his house, and people began to come to him with terrible news. All of his sheep, cattle and camels were stolen. A house fell on all of his children and they were killed. Job fell to the ground with heavy sadness.

"I came into the world a naked baby, and I will go out a naked old man. Blessed be God."

God said, "See he is good. He did not curse me."

Satan said, "No he is not…he lost a lot, but he wasn't hurt. Let's see what happens if he is in pain."

God agreed.

Job grew sick. He had disgusting sores all over his body. He itched and burned. He couldn't sleep or move without pain.

His wife said, "Curse God and die."

Job said, "No. We accept good from God so why not accept what is bad."

Three friends came to be with him in his misery. They sat with him, but then they thought God must be punishing him.

Job said, "No. I am a good person, even if I hurt and am sad. I will curse the day I was born, but not God."

MOVEMENTS	WORDS
	His friends thought he was lying. They said he must have done something bad. Job said that his friends were unkind.
Add the fourth friend.	A fourth person came. He was very young. and became angry. He said he had been afraid to speak, but now in his anger he wanted Job to know that Job was wrong. "You must have done something bad. You just don't know what it is."
*Place **Object #4** (whirlwind) on the underlay.*	Suddenly a whirlwind came across the fields towards them. Job heard God's voice in its terrible turning.

God said, "Where were you when I created the earth? What do you know about my ways?"

Job said, "I have no more to say." |
| ***Object #5:** Hold the fish hook over the underlay as you mention the fish hook and then put it down.* | God went on: "Can you lift up the Leviathon, a great beast, like a little fish on a hook?" |
| *Lift up the piece of string and pantomime pushing the string against the tongue of a Leviathan.* | "Can you push down its tongue with a little piece of limp string?"

Job said, "I have tried to say things too wonderful for me to know. I still know nothing about your ways, but now I know you."

God was angry with the friends of Job and told them they also did not know what they were talking about. Now they needed to say they were sorry to Job and to God. |
| ***Object #6:** Recreate the first scene; place the second square of green felt on the underlay; place Job, Mrs. Job and the five new children on the green felt (but no animals).* | Job lived for many more years. His sores healed and he grew rich again. His family grew once more. He accepted all of this. He took no credit for it, because he had met God face to face and that is what mattered. |

MOVEMENTS

WORDS

COMPLETE LAYOUT OF THE STORY OF JOB (CHILDREN'S PERSPECTIVE)

Sit for a moment and look at the lesson from beginning to end to let the story rest. Then begin the wondering.

I wonder what part of this story you liked the best?

I wonder what part was the most important?

I wonder what part was about you, or what part you were in?

I wonder if we could leave any of the story out and still have all the story that we need?

After the wondering is over, put the story away carefully. Pick up each object in reverse order and remind the children what the object is, saying for example, "Here is the fish hook..." After all of the objects are back in the tray, carefully model how to roll the underlay back up and place it in the tray as well. Return the lesson to its place on the shelf. Then return to your spot in the circle and dismiss the children one by one to their work.

OTHER TITLES AND VIDEOS IN THIS SERIES

THE COMPLETE GUIDE TO GODLY PLAY
BY JEROME W. BERRYMAN

An imaginative method for presenting scripture stories to children

This five-volume series invites preschool through 6th grade children to discover God, themselves and one another through our sacred stories. Based on Jerome Berryman's work in the Montessori tradition, *Godly Play* uses a careful telling of scripture stories, engaging story figures and activities to encourage children to seek and find answers to their faith questions. *Godly Play* respects the innate spirituality of children and encourages curiosity and imagination in experiencing the mystery and joy of God.

HERE'S WHAT YOU GET IN EACH VOLUME:

VOLUME 1: How to Lead *Godly Play* Lessons contains all of the material you will need to be familiar with the *Godly Play* approach, including how to create a special space for children, plan and present the lesson and help children develop spiritually. 978-1-8891-0895-7

VOLUME 2: Fall - includes opening lesson on the church year followed by 13 Old Testament stories, from Creation through the prophets. 978-1-8891-0896-4

VOLUME 3: Winter - includes 20 presentations based on stories about Advent and the feasts of Christmas & Epiphany, followed by the parables. 978-1-8891-0897-1

VOLUME 4: Spring - presents 20 lessons covering stories of Lent, the resurrection, the Eucharist and the early Church during Easter Season. 978-1-8891-0898-8

VOLUME 5: Practical Helps from Godly Play Trainers - experienced trainers and teachers share insights, stories and ideas for using *Godly Play* to its fullest. 978-1-9319-6004-5

VOLUME 6: Enrichment Sessions - 15 new presentations with focus on the Old Testament People of God, created to integrate with the presentations in Volume 2, including Abraham, Sarah, Moses and Ruth. 978-1-9319-6042-7

VOLUME 7: Enrichment Sessions - 12 new lessons focusing on the saints, including Nicholas, Julian of Norwich, Augustine, Teresa of Avila and many more! 978-1-9319-6046-5

COMING SOON!

VOLUME 8: Additional Enrichment Sessions - new lessons with focus on stories of Jesus, including Lent and the resurrection appearances of Jesus.

HOW-TO DVDS

Masterful *Godly Play* storyteller Jerome W. Berryman guides catechists through two actual *Godly Play* sessions per season. In this three-part series, listeners are enthusiastically engaged in how to tell the story and invite children to experience the wondering.

Available in VHS & DVD formats

To purchase these products, contact your local bookstore or call Morehouse Education Resources at 1-800-242-1918.

www.morehouseeducation.org

THE COMPLETE GUIDE TO GODLY PLAY	
VOLUMES 1-8	**$ 24.95 each**

Sessions are adaptable from 45 minutes to 2 hours and include a complete materials list. 8¼" x 10¾", 120 pages, paperback

FALL VHS OR DVD	**$ 24.95 each**
WINTER VHS OR DVD	**$ 24.95 each**
SPRING VHS OR DVD	**$ 24.95 each**

Approximately 45 min. each.